ALIVE IN KRISHNA

To My Darling
Chote Bhai
Amal -

From your Mota Bhaiyya -
Love & Blessings

[illegible]

11/3/00

page 38
1+2 paragraphs

ALIVE in KRISHNA

Ghanshyamdas Birla

PARAGON HOUSE

NEW YORK

The following have been of valuable help to me, and I therefore extend my grateful thanks to: the commentaries of Swami Chinmayananda in the Gita and Upanishads; Lokmanya Tilak's "Gita Rahasya"; the abridged "Bhagavat" rendered in Gujarati by Gopaldas Jivabhai Patel; the abridged "Mahabharata" in English by Kamala Subramaniam; "Krishna's Life" in Bangali by Bankim Babu; and the numerous devotional verses of the godly. I should also thankfully acknowledge my obligation to Kamala Subramaniam for this English version of the original work in Hindi.

Paintings reproduced courtesy of the Birla Academy of Art and Culture and of Basant Kumar Birla.

Library of Congress Cataloging-in-Publication Data

Biralâ, Ghanásyámadása, 1894–1983.
Alive in Krishna.
1. Translation of: Krishnam vande jagadgurum.
1. Krishna (Hindu deity). 2. Bhagavadgíta—Criticism, interpretation, etc. I. Title.
BL1220.B5513 1986 294.5'211 86–4936
ISBN 0–913757–65–9 (pbk.)

Published by Paragon House Publishers
2 Hammarskjold Plaza
New York, New York 10017

Introduction

This book is a strategic choice for inclusion in the series Patterns of World Spirituality. For it reveals how classical Hindu spirituality nourished the life of one of the most influential men of 20th century India. It dispels the Western misconception that Hindu spirituality is intrinsically other-worldly—that it ascends so single-mindedly into the transcendent as to abandon all concern for the material dimensions of life. On the contrary, in this book we see a man, steeped in the spirituality of the ancient sacred texts of India, who through his practical genius shaped one of the great industrial complexes of the contemporary world. At the same time he presents a model that challenges the West, for in developing his industry he did not fall into the trap of materialism. These pages reveal, rather, a radiant soul who gives primacy to the spiritual and who draws from that realm the inspiration and energy for transforming the material world.

G.D. Birla was heir to an industrial tradition that had its beginnings in the nineteenth century when his grandfather Seth Shivanarain Birla set out from the small town of Pilani, in the deserts of Rajastan in Western India to seek his fortune. From his work the House of Birla was born and was later consolidated by his son Raja Baldeodas Birla. In the twentieth century it was Shri Ghanshyamdas Birla who shaped the destiny of the House of Birla, developing it into one of Asia's major commercial and industrial empires, which extends from India to Indonesia, Malaysia, South Korea, Thailand, the Philippines, and farther. The industry processes and produces a broad spectrum of products, including: pulp, textiles, cotton and rayon, chemicals, automobiles, engineering equipment, electrical power, aluminum, cement, and rubber products. Through the years the House of Birla has been one of India's largest and most successful industrial complexes, vying with that of the Tatas for the top position in India. Taking into account many differences, one can compare the Birlas in India to the Fords and Rockefellers in the United States.

Through the years the Birlas have been leading philanthropists in India, building schools, technological and research centers in the family seat of Pilani; the Birla Academy of Art in Calcutta and the Central Museum in Pilani; and temples throughout India, like the great Lakshmi-Narayan Temple in Delhi.

As is clear from this book, G.D. Birla saw his personal and public life from a spiritual perspective. A decisive influence on him was his long association with Mahatma Gandhi, who was his personal spiritual guide. He followed Gandhi's teachings and supported his work in many ways. During much of the last year of his life, Gandhi lived in G.D. Birla's home in Delhi. In fact, it was in the garden of this home that Gandhi was assassinated in 1948. The site, including the garden and the house, has been turned into a national monument and museum. Birla lived a life of service, *karma* yoga, with a complete dedication of his energies to human and spiritual values. In accordance with the teaching of Gandhi, the wealth that he had inherited and which he increased through his genius, he held, in radical detachment, as a sacred trust to be used for the good of his fellow human beings.

This is not an autobiography in the conventional meaning of the term, for G. D. Birla does not tell the story of the external events of his life. What he has written is a spiritual autobiography, but in a special sense. For it is not the journal of a soul's spiritual quest laid out in narrative form like the *Confessions* of Augustine. Rather it is his meditations on the sources of Hindu spirituality, especially the great Indian epic the *Mahabharata*, of which the *Bhagavadgita* is a part. He draws the reader into that central point in his soul where the great spiritual writings of Hinduism nourish his life. Like the Ganges, this vast tradition flows into his life from its source in the *Vedas*, in the later currents of the *Upanisads*, the great epics of the *Ramayana* and the *Mahabharata* with the *Bhagavadgita*. To use another image, the book serves as a mirror, reflecting both the wisdom of the Hindu tradition and the interior spiritual life of G.D. Birla as he allows this wisdom to shine in his life.

At first the Western reader may find himself or herself lost in the array of names and incidents which we do not share in our cultural memory. However, Birla has the gift of drawing us into the universal values that transcend our cultural and religious differences. Behind the level of alien facts there lies a deeper difference. Unlike the West, the Hindu tradition has incorporated into its spiritual literature the great epics of its heroic age. Although the Bible contains elements of an heroic age, our own epics are drawn from Greek sources which have not been assimilated into our sacred literature. Imagine, by way of comparison, that the *Iliad* and *Odyssey* were considered sacred poems and that the New Testament, the West's equivalent of the *Bhagavadgita*, were embedded in the *Iliad*.

One does not have to travel far in India or remain long to observe how alive these epics are in the religious experience of all levels of Hindu society. They are chanted, sung, dramatized in dance, and depicted in art. This means that the Hindu is much more adept than the Westerner in perceiving spiritual meaning in a corpus of literature that employs epic narrative forms and mythic imagination. By entering with G.D. Birla into the very heart of this literature, the reader can share a rich "pattern of world spirituality" and awaken faculties of spiritual perception that have lain dormant in the West.

It was my privilege to meet G.D. Birla personally in January of 1983, only a few months before his death. I had been enjoying the hospitality of his son B.K. and his daughter-in-law, Sarala, as often on my previous trips to Calcutta. On this occasion they invited me to attend a program on the spiritual meaning of the epic poem the *Ramayana*, as expounded by a famous pandit. At the climax of the program, G.D. Birla gave an exposition on the spiritual meaning of the *Ramayana* before the hundreds of distinguished Indians in the audience, who were visibly moved by the depth of his spiritual wisdom.

When he learned that I had never met his father, B.K. invited me to come to the family home the next morning to discuss with his father his relation with Gandhi. From the moment G.D. Birla entered the room, I felt that I was in the presence of "a great soul"—which is the meaning of the term "Mahatma" that Tagore had applied to Gandhi and which became his popular name. As G.D. Birla described Gandhi's teaching and his personal influence on his life, I realized that here was a man who in his own way had reached a depth of spirituality from which his "great soul" could be manifest. It is this greatness of soul that shines through each page of his book.

At the time of my visit, the Birla family was having a documentary film made on their father's life. Since the cameraman was on hand, B.K. had him film my interview with his father. On another visit to the Birlas the following year—after the father's death—I saw the completed film. It featured the pilgrimage the father had made, in the last year of his life, to Gangotri, the source of the Ganges in the Himalayas. Although he was in his late eighties at the time, he insisted on walking up the snow-covered trail of this classical pilgrim path into the mountains. This final pilgrimage was a symbol of his life, for his many decades of dedicated activity constituted a spiritual journey.

This pilgrimage had another symbolic meaning, for he was returning to the source of the Ganges—that symbol of the rich spiritual heritage of India which flows so abundantly through the classics of Hinduism. It was from this source that his life was nourished. The reader of his book will find on each page the confluence of these two symbolic meanings: his own spiritual journey as it intersects and is enriched by the classical spiritual tradition of Hinduism.

Ewert Cousins

वसुदेवसुतं देवं
कंसचाणूरमर्दनम्
देवकीपरमानन्दं
कृष्णं वंदे जगद्गुरुम् ।

I salute Krishna, the Teacher of the Universe, the Divine son of Vasudeva, the destroyer of Kamsa and Chamura, the supreme joy of Devaki.

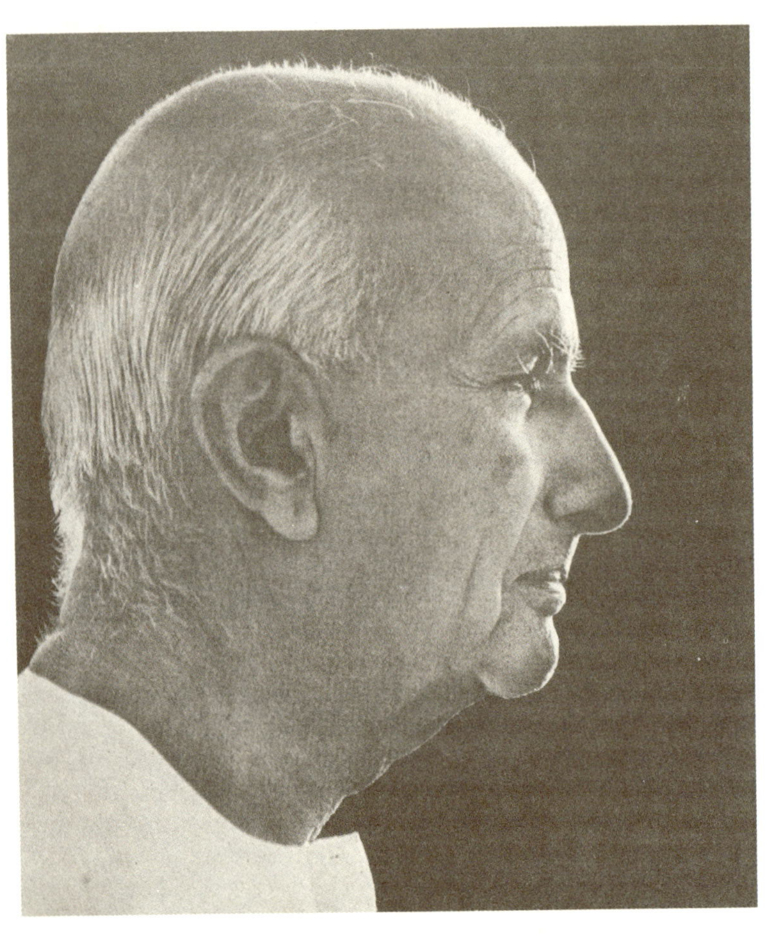

Ghanshyamdas Birla

વિષ્ણુર્વા ત્રિપુરાંતકો ભવતુ વા
બ્રહ્મા સુરેન્દ્રોઽથવા
ભાનુર્વા શશલક્ષણોઽથ ભગવાન્
બુદ્ધોઽથ સિદ્ધોઽથવા ।
રાગદ્વેષવિષાર્તિમોહરહિતઃ
સત્વાનુકમ્પોદ્યતો
યઃ સર્વૈઃ સહ સંસ્કૃતો ગુણગણૈઃ
તસ્મૈ નમઃ સર્વદા ॥

May He be Vishnu or Shiva, the Destroyer of the three cities;
May He be Brahma, The Creator or Indra, the Celestial Lord;
May He be the Sun God or the Moon, by hare-like mark distinguished;
Or Buddha, the Enlightened or Siddha (Lord Mahavira), the Accomplished;

Our salutations ever be to Him who is free from the delusion wrought by the afflictions of the poison of passion and hatred, who actively showers compassion on all creatures; and who is rendered perfect by the possession of all the host of virtues.

Looking Back

Quite sometime back, I wrote down some of my reminiscences. As far as I can remember, there was no particular reason for this effort, no immediate cause. It was just one of those things one does to please oneself and I had set down these few "Memories" as they came to my mind. There was no method nor any order in this collection. They were just stray moments from the past strung together, perhaps, with the thread of memory. This book, which I had written in Hindi, was printed and published. Strangely enough, several people who happened to read it seemed to have enjoyed the book.

I have stated that there was no particular reason which prompted me to write the book. But now, when I look back, I am not quite so sure if that statement was wholly correct. There are some thoughts, some emotions, some reflections which lie buried deep in the mind and we do not seem to be aware of their existence unless and until they rise up to the level of consciousness from the buried depths.

The mind is indeed fascinating. It cannot be brought under complete control nor can it be said that one knows what goes on in one's mind. No one can say confidently that he knows his own mind. It is like a bird which can fly at will wherever it pleases. It flits from thought to thought with so much swiftness that the man himself cannot guess whereto it will stray next! No man can gauge the thoughts which are still unknown to him, unexpressed. Nor can he give expression to the many desires which again lie deep down in his mind: thoughts which make the mind flounder here and there, with no reins to hold it back or to quieten it. Unless he is familiar with every quiver of the wings of the mind, every aspect of this mercurial substance, man cannot have peace.

All this speculation makes me wonder if, unknown to me, some inner desire prompted me to set down my reminiscences on paper. I am still wondering.

There is one particular weakness which is common to all those who are old. They revel in going over their past. They enjoy taking up some glowing moments from the days of long ago, turn them in their old hands with infinite care and live those moments all over again. There is a reason behind this.

When a man is nearing the sunset of his life he realizes all of a sudden that there is no more future to which he can look forward. What confronts him now is but a sheer blank wall, a dark veil hanging in space. What is beyond it is something which his senses cannot comprehend. Poised as he is at the very bourne of life, man is completely ignorant of the truth on the other side of the veil. And so, whatever knowledge he has is what he has been able to garner during his pilgrimage through the years. Thus it is but natural for him to look back and derive some kind of pleasure in trying to live it all over again by remembering it.

When he was living his earlier life, when the past he is now looking at was the present, these years held for him the hopes and thrills of a future which was yet to unfold before him. But now this same future is lost in the abyss of Time. What is left for him is just a memory of the pageant of past events and a very doubtful, indistinct and uncertain present which is, by its very nature, extremely limited, hovering as it does on the brink of the horizon. There is nothing left to look forward to any more, nothing to get excited about.

Looking back, one's youth, which has been left behind long ago, seems so different! It was then filled to the brim with dreams, hopes and aspirations about the endless future which was lying ahead. The world was his oyster. Lost in dreams of happiness, man had time for nothing but the thrill of anticipation.

The contrast between the mental makeup of an elder and that of a youngster is as sharp and clear as that between night and day. The youth has the future which is yet to come while the elder knows that it has already come and gone. He is no longer able to build his hopes on the days to come since there are but a few left. And yet, even *he* has to have some pleasure, some moments of thrill. This he is able to achieve by looking back and resting his mind lovingly on the many events that have happened during his early life and he is happy once again. He is like a painter. The artist has produced and completed his work of art. He steps back now from the easel, scans the canvas and touches it up here and there with more color. He tries to enhance the beauty of the picture and he thus derives a pleasure, a fulfillment which is unique in its own way. Again and again he touches up the canvas with his tinted brush, all the time considering, contemplating if the embellishment blends with the total landscape.

All these thoughts crowd my mind since I am no longer the youngster I once was. And that, perhaps, was the motivation behind my writing my "Reminscences".

Whatever might have been the reason, the book was written and it did please those who read it. And they asked me, suggested to me that I should make an attempt to write out my autobiography!

The Ego

The suggestion of my friends set in motion a new train of thought. Granted that I agree to write about myself, the problem was , which "I" should be the hero of my book?

I was once a boy, naive and innocent. Later came my youth. Then followed the process of growing older and finally, the setting in of old age. The birth of one stage in one's life is, naturally, the death of the previous one. The child dies and the boy is born. The boy vanishes to make way for the youth and so it goes on. Reckoned thus, I have had several deaths and I have been born just as many times.

And again, at times I have been well, at times ill. There have been days when I was totally at peace with the entire world and at other times restless and worried. Different feelings and different emotions colored the many moments and they have formed a continuous but passing pageant against the screen which was my "past" life. Now, when I consider all these factors, which "I" from these many instances should I select as the subject for my "autobiography"?

One thing seems to be certain. When a man makes up his mind to write about himself, he should have a mind which is tranquil. If he is "at war with himself", how can he do justice to the task which he undertakes? Perhaps my arguments may seem to some as hair-splitting, but I am helpless.

This question has not ceased to bother me and, unless I solve it, I may not be able to proceed further.

Another question arises seeking an immediate answer. What is the purpose behind this attempt to write the story of one's life? Is it purely to entertain? Some of my friends told me that the story of my life would be a guide post to the young. To an extent, I do grant that the book might prove to be a source of entertainment. As for the idea, however, that my life could be an example to be followed, it would be sheer foolishness if I accept it.

Entertainment and instruction are, to my mind, poles apart. They can never be coupled together. It is possible to recollect only the pleasant experiences of the past and to recount them to others. And again if the aim is solely to entertain oneself, it is possible to do so. But it is evident that such a narrative must be lacking in depth, in seriousness. The disappointments, heartbreaks, difficulties, hardships, the painful moments which are best forgotten—all these are not the materials to be used if the book has to be entertaining. They may serve as warnings, perhaps, but they do not make the writer happy while relating them.

The purpose in one instance is quite different from the other. I may be able to amuse people, perhaps, but the other purpose can never be achieved. I am extremely diffident and I do not believe in thinking that my life will be a source of inspiration to the coming generations.

It seems to me, however, that the respect and affection which people may have for the writer should be considered carefully by him. If he is foolish enough to agree with them and tells himself that what they say is true, that he owes it to humanity to recount the story of his life so that it may profit by it, he is only deceiving himself. The value he places on his individual life is entirely false.

Pandit Madan Mohan Malaviya was an evolved soul and his way of life has had a great influence on me, my thinking, and my life. He was a saintly person, a man of infinite patience, great intellect and great character. I felt that such a man, endowed as he was with so many great qualities, was an example to be emulated. Once, when I was talking to him,

I said: "Panditji, you should write the story of your life."

He replied: "Ghanshyamji, if you wish to read the life story of anyone, then the book to be studied is the Bhagavata. What is so great about my life that it should be worthwhile studying it?"

His words, like an arrow shot by a master archer, pierced into the innermost recesses of my heart and have lodged there ever since.

He spoke nothing but the truth. If the aim is to know the life of someone and then to follow in the path traced out by him, then study the lives of the numerous exemplary characters in our epics. These ancient books are full of such lives and for thousands of years people have been reading them and have benefited by them.

Vyasa edited the Vedas and, later, based on that, composed the Mahabharata. He followed it up with the Bhagavata. All these had but one purpose, the well-being of humanity.

One significant fact should be noted very carefully. Vyasa has written about many great men but never once has he spoken a word about himself. Maybe there was no one to approach him with the suggestion that he should write about himself! If such an event had taken place, Vyasa's reply would surely have been the same as Malaviyaji's.

If we consider the great literature of the past, one fact stands out: no one has any knowledge of the authors. Vyasa has not told us anything about himself. We do not know about the giant intellects responsible for the Upanishads. We know them as Ishavasya, Kena, Mandukya or Prasna and that is all we know. This effacement of self, this anonymity is a precedent set up by the great ones since time immemorial and it has been followed faithfully by the later Acharyas like Bhagavan Buddha, Adi Sankara, Ramanuja or Madhva. Even the great souls of comparatively recent times, bhaktas like Tulsi, Kabir and Mira have not spoken about themselves.

This habit of "blowing one's own trumpet" has come into force only recently, during the last century and a half, perhaps.

It is necessary to say a word more about those who write about themselves. In their writings is present a touch of hypocrisy. It may be subconscious, perhaps, but it is still there. The author presents for the benefit of the reader a very charming, attractive portrayal of himself which is neither quite true nor quite honest.

Of course the reader is not a fool and he is not deceived all that easily. But, strangely enough, the writer seems to be quite unaware of this! He deludes himself with the thought that anything he says will be believed. He pushes his weaknesses and infirmities discreetly into the background, out of sight. And the ordinary commonplace virtues or characteristics are placed right in the foreground.

If the writer thinks that such a book will prove to be a "lodestar" for those poor mortals floundering in the sea of suffering, he is completely under a delusion.

About Biographies

In the West, in Europe and America for instance, biographies have been written about famous people. Attempts have been made to make these biographies true to life. The good and bad characteristics of the person have both been included and there is placed before us a complete picture of him or her. We become fully acquainted with the person's strengths as well as weaknesses.

Such books, to my mind, do not seem to be adequate. They are but books of the hour, of the times when the person lived. They may prove interesting during a span of time but after that they become antique, outdated and important only as chronicles—and even then of interest to only a few.

Consider Sir Winston Churchill. I knew him well and he has been one of the few who have influenced my thinking. Men like him are not born every day. I was very close to him, or so I thought until I read his biography written by his physician. Then I realized that there was a face of Churchill to which I was a stranger. In this biography Lord Moran, the author, has not hesitated to write about the many weaknesses of the man. The book is highly instructive but it does not claim to be eternal.

Roosevelt was another powerful personality of recent times. In his biography, they tell us, for instance, that he was not faithful to his wife. This fact is shocking, according to our moral code, and it takes time to accept it.

The point I am trying to drive home is merely this: where great people are concerned, these facts should not be considered all that important. This human body, this bundle of bones and flesh cannot but help being a home of strength and weakness at the same time. When we think of the lives of some of the sages of ancient times we hear that they have also succumbed to the weakness of the flesh. As the poet so aptly puts it, like the swans which take only the milk leaving the water behind, even so should we deal with the nature of man. We should learn to ignore the weak traits. Once again I claim that it would have been different if these two had written their stories themselves. Most probably they would have suppressed their faults and we would never have known the truth about them.

If we try to sum up the ultimate gain from these biographies, they satisfy our curiosity about these people. Once that purpose is served their place is the bookshelf and the chances of their being reread are very few as there is nothing of permanent value in these books.

There is another class of beings who revel in laying bare their innermost thoughts, their weaknesses, their moral lapses, and get a thrill out of these revelations. Rousseau is the name which comes to my mind. This French writer has set down his "Confessions". To the Indian mind, steeped in a peculiar culture of its own, Rousseau's book with its vivid descriptions of his many "affairs" seems strange. It is a mystery as to what prompts such as he to write these books. Some mental unrest, perhaps, must have been responsible.

Alexander, Julius Caesar, Hannibal, Attila, are some famous names in history and their biographies have been written by scholars who have spent a lot of time over them. These books are about men in the distant past and, naturally, one wonders how much they are true to life. The same is true of Napoleon, Hitler or Mussolini.

These books, however, serve one purpose. They serve as warnings to mankind: how men intoxicated with power had tried to rule the world by force. They lost sight of the dividing line between right and wrong and misused their power. The reader draws his own conclusion that ultimately evil cannot triumph. Our sacred books have repeated this truth over and over, again and again, and history has proved it.

As for the lives of great souls like Socrates or St. Francis of Assisi, while most of the details are but heresay and cannot be proved, the words spoken by these men have stood the test of time.

When we consider the lives of bhaktas like Tulsidas, Surdas, Mira, Sant Tukaram, Samarth Ramadas, Jnanadev and others, the words they have spoken serve as commentaries on their lives. Their aim was the welfare of mankind. They wanted to make man conscious of the goodness in him. They did not waste their time and energy in writing about themselves and this is proof of their disinterest in worldly fame.

Summing up, this long dissertation goes to prove that different types of people have written biographies prompted by different motives. Lives of men like Alexander only serve to bring home the truth that might has never been successful in suppressing the spirit of man, and that evil will not go unpunished.

Chronicles of Good and Bad

It has to be granted however that we cannot entirely ignore these biographies. If, for instance, a man is fired with an ambition to become a great leader, a soldier, these books then serve as incentives to him. For a person who wants to amass wealth, it will be profitable to pore over the lives of Henry Ford or Andrew Carnegie.

But I still maintain that this type of literature is not lasting. Why? The very purpose which spurred these "heroes" was worldly and temporal. This is why this kind of writing has not found a place in Indian literature. Our wise men have not been indifferent to victory in war or to the accumulation of wealth at any time. No. Only they have obeyed a stipulated condition that these should be for the welfare of mankind. Plain greed or avarice should not be the reason for establishing a kingdom or for becoming rich. The acquisition of wealth for selfish reasons does not win the approbation of the wise and so should be avoided.

There is a vast difference between the great war fought on the field of Kurukshetra and the world war that was caused by Hitler. One was fought because of the evil thoughts in the minds of men and its purpose was the annihilation of a segment of mankind, while the other was so noble that Krishna himself took the reins of Arjuna's chariot in his blessed hand and taught mankind the philosophy of Karma yoga.

If a man is to be remembered long after he is gone, his life should be a dedicated one. He should have found fulfillment in his service to mankind. His name will then be etched on the Scrolls of Time. Our literature recounts the stories of such men and it has stood the test of time.

In the stories about men like Socrates, their words have been carefully preserved. These words spoken by the great men of the past help to rouse the goodness in the hearts of all men.

Let us consider the photograph of a man or woman. By and large, the picture is true to life and realistic. And yet, the artist looks askance at the photographer. According to him photography is not an art. He feels that a photograph, the two dimensional likeness of a person, cannot be the portrayal of the entire person.

Man is made up of the five elements blended in such a way that they gain form and features and this is the physical man. But that does not quite complete the picture. Along with the physical, there is something else, something vital, which is essential for a man to be what he is. This vital factor is the Atman. A complete man is made up of three essentials—Adibhautika, Adidaivika and Adhyatmika. A picture of just the physical features of a man does not and cannot do justice to the entirety that is man. That is why, in his portrayal of his subject, the artist tries to bring out this "Soul" of man.

This is exactly what the sages of old tried when they drew for us a picture of the Lord. The descriptions of the physical body are scanty and not adequate enough to bring before our eyes a picture of the man as he might have looked. They took particular care to elaborate on his qualities, on his character, and make him more memorable because of these than because of the descriptions of him.

Krishna comes to the mind at once. His beauty, his charm, his attractive form have all been mentioned. The colorful peacock feather which he was wont to sport on his locks, the yellow silk which draped him are familiar to us. To me, Krishna's complexion has always been a source of mystery. They say he was dark; that he was like a dark blue lotus;

that he was colored like a rain-bearing cloud. All these epithets do not seem natural.

The poets have left it mostly to the imagination of the reader and they have concentrated on giving us the character in great detail. Vyasa and Tulsi have succeeded in this art of bringing to our minds the subject and his qualities which are worthy of admiration, and Kalidasa has followed in their footsteps. In his portrayal of Raghu, stress is laid on his achievements rather than on his appearance.

It is worth repeating what has been said before: the aim of the authors of the past was the well-being of the world. They drew the attention of the reader to the greatness of the Lord and they tried to kindle Bhakti in the heart of the reader, to lead him on to the right path.

Returning to the man who aspires to write the story of his life, no man, after all this speculation, will have the audacity to consider that he is so important that he should tell the world about himself! And this is why I maintain that the words of Malaviyaji are gospel truth: that one should study the Bhagavata. "Study the Bhagavata *and* the Mahabharata," I would add.

When the sacred river Ganga is within reach who will quench his thirst in a filthy pond? When great literature is there for the asking, why should one waste one's time reading the books of the hour, books which are of no lasting value?

Bhagavata Dharma

The book one should read is the Bhagavata. Let us go back to the Vedas, the ancient fountainhead of all learning. There is something eternal about the Vedas. It is beyond the span of human conjecture as to when they came into existence or which brain conceived them. One can only generalize. The word "Ved" means "to know" and knowledge is eternal, perennial, and it needs no author. To use a modern analogy, the fact that Benjamin Franklin and Thomas Edison revealed the existence of electricity to the world does not mean that it was created by them. It had been there always and it was "discovered" by them. And so, the Vedas.

According to the shastras, to Bhagavan Vyasa goes the entire credit of collecting the Vedas, editing them and compiling them into the Samhitas. As a consequence of this stupendous effort of Vyasa, the Vedas became more accessible to the world of ordinary human beings.

And yet, after the completion of the task he had undertaken, Vyasa could not derive the satisfaction which comes with a great achievement. He thought about it and realized that the bulk of the Vedas was beyond the comprehension of a large section of society in spite of the immense trouble he had taken to simplify it and make it easy to understand. Vyasa wanted to propagate Dharma and many of the people were not well-versed enough to understand the Vedas. He wanted to make them easy and simple enough to be understood by the ordinary man and so he withdrew to a solitary spot—Badari—and there he composed the great epic Mahabharata. Jaya was the name given to the poem. Later, the name Bharata came into vogue and, in the course of time, this gained in size and volume and became the Mahabharata.

So far, no one has disputed the fact that this great epic is a unique creation. Here is found a happy blending of Vedanta and the philosophy of daily life. The rules of Dharma, of justice, of worldly living, of statecraft, can all be found here. There is a fanciful concept of the poet that when weighed against the Mahabharata the Vedas were found to be wanting. The idea may be fanciful but there is more than a grain of truth in it. Vyasa himself has told us that it contains the many nuances of Dharma. Many are familiar with the saying: "What is found in the Mahabharata can be found here and there in other great compositions but with great difficulty. However, what is not in the Mahabharata is nowhere to be found."

In his journey through life a traveler has to encounter myriads of difficulties, face many ordeals, take up any number of challenges. When such situations arise it is good to fall back upon the Mahabharata and consider the great characters and their reactions to the trials they had to face. The manner in which they solved the many problems which beset them cannot but be an example to any human being. This reward can be gleaned from other poems and other teachers, but with great effort, while it is easily understood in the Mahabharata.

The Mahabharata is such a wonderful epic, such an exquisite work of art that no other work can equal it, be it in Sanskrit or in any other language. In the journey through life there is no greater help than the Mahabharata, the great storehouse of wisdom.

What is the core of the teachings of the great epic? It is the Bhagavata dharma or the Narayaniya dharma as it has been called. At the conclusion of the Shanti Parva this lesson has been taught in great detail. In the Gita, Vyasa declares that in ancient times Vivasvan Manu, Ikshvaku and others were familiar with this dharma which had been forgotten due to the passage of time.

When the threat of its disappearance seemed imminent, Vyasa infused new life into it. The credit for this renascence goes to Bhagavan Sri Krishna. This is the reason why it is the custom to salute Nara, Narayana, Vyasa and Sarasvati before beginning the study of the Mahabharata.

नारायणं नमस्कृत्य नरं चैव नरोत्तमं ।
देवीं सरस्वतीं व्यासं ततो जयमुदीरयेत् ॥

This is the Dhyana sloka of the Mahabharata.

Bhakti, the Easy Path to a Richer Life

The names Nara and Narayana, which occur in the sloka which is recited at the beginning of the study of the great epic, are the names of two great rishis of ancient times who were born again as Krishna and Arjuna. The purpose of their birth was the resurrection of the Bhagavata dharma.

This Bhagavata dharma is none other than the path of Pravritti—action without any desire tainting it: the path which goes by the name of Karma yoga in the Bhagavad Gita. In the Shanti Parva we find the words: "Narayana is the ultimate dharma. It saves you from the eternal cycle of births and deaths." Pravritti marga has Narayana as the guiding principle.

What is this Pravritti marga? In essence it is this. There is no need to adopt sanyasa, no need to renounce the world, to sever the bonds of kith and kin. Man should live in the world and continue with his duties, BUT, at the same time there should be this one thought in his mind always, that no selfish desires should contaminate the purity of his actions. With disinterestedness, with no thought for any return or reward, man should act in the world solely because it is his duty to do so. No man should avoid action. If he should do so, he will be shirking his responsibilities.

Bhagavata dharma advocates Pravritti which is but a synonym for Nishkama karma or Karma yoga. At the time of the Mahabharata Krishna reestablished this dharma which seemed in danger of being lost in the mists of oblivion.

When we consider the Bhagavata, we find that this is again a guide post for the propagation of dharma. But there is one vital difference between the two great works. In the Mahabharata, emphasis is laid on Karma yoga and Bhakti finds a secondary place in its scheme. Here, too, as in the Gita, Pravritti marga is spoken of and the path of renunciation is not advocated. But the emphasis here is on Bhakti. Studying these two poems one gets a clear picture of the yogas, Karma and Bhakti. The Gita emphasizes the truth that these two yogas are complementary and tells us also that both are pathways to the third yoga, the Jnana yoga, the search after the Ultimate Truth. Karma and Bhakti are so well mingled with Jnana that we can see all three of them as a comprehensive whole. This is the peculiar greatness of the Gita.

In spite of this total view of the several pathways, it is evident that in the Gita stress is laid on Karma yoga, with this special observance that there is not much difference between Karma and Bhakti yogas. The Gita is part of the Mahabharata and both of them are invaluable as incentives for the practice of Karma yoga, of the Pravritti marga.

Strangely enough, Vyasa was not entirely satisfied with himself even after he had composed the Mahabharata, because even this simplified epic was still difficult for the ordinary man to understand. Men, he found, were not able to grasp the significance of the lesson of the epic.

It is a fact that we are quite ignorant of the people who constituted the society of those days. And yet, it seems as though the society during that era too had strayed far from the path of truth and righteousness and was floundering in the darkness of ignorance—Avidya. There seems to have arisen a need for a new code, some new teaching which could bring society back to the path of righteousness, to help raise it from the depths to which it had fallen. As for the Vedas, they were inaccessible to and beyond the mental reach of the average man. This was when the priests came into the picture. They began to insist that the performance of different types of yajnas was the duty of man and this was the means, the only means, to salvation.

The Mahabharata was, no doubt, an incomparable storehouse, a treasury of teaching about the right way of living. It was couched in easy and simple language. And yet all men could not comprehend the core of its teachings, the purpose underlying the poem.

When Vyasa observed this, he felt that he should compose yet another poem which would be even more easy to understand than the Mahabharata. He wanted the poem to be such that the ordinary man could study it with his limited knowledge and intelligence, and benefit by it. It should help him to view his daily life and conduct in an entirely new light and help him to rise out of the morass into which he seemed to have fallen.

Vyasa spoke about this dissatisfaction to the sage Narada. He said: "My lord, I do not seem to find any happiness or peace even after having completed the Mahabharata."

Narada replied: "My friend, you have done a great service to mankind by your great work which is meant to teach mankind the observance of dharma. To an extent you have gained your objective. BUT, in the Mahabharata you have, again and again, laid emphasis on the importance of Karma yoga. During the process you have ignored, to an extent, the path which goes by the name Bhakti.

"Remember this, my friend. An ordinary man has not the strength of mind, the intelligence, the introspection which are essential for the understanding and assimilation of higher thoughts, nor is he able to follow the path traced out for him. And so, for such a man, a man who is not evolved enough, how is it possible to learn anything from the study of the great characters in the Mahabharata and how can he try to emulate them in his daily life? How will he be able to discriminate between what should be done and what should not?

"For the benefit of such simple-minded men there is but one answer and that is Bhakti. The lowest of the low is certain to benefit by the path of Bhakti and to become evolved. This path is extremely simple to follow. There is no obstacle placed in the path of Bhakti: it is easy. I suggest that you compose a poem whose sole theme is Bhakti, which will kindle the interest of the simplest of men and plant in his mind a desire to pursue the path of Bhakti which will lead to the Lord."

Vyasa considered this suggestion of Narada, accepted the truth of it and composed the Bhagavata.

Bhajan and Kirtan

The date of the Bhagavata is not known and it is still a matter of controversy. It can safely be said that it existed fifteen hundred years ago, perhaps even earlier than that.

Like the other poem of Vyasa, the Bhagavata also lays stress on the Bhagavata. This dharma is attributed solely to Krishna. People were familiar with it two thousands years ago but, though scholars have elaborated on it, it is not so easily understood in present times.

At the time when these two poems were composed there was a dearth of Dharma. Men paid scant attention to the contemplation of the Atman which is the core of the teachings of Vedanta. The priests held sway over the multitude and, in their hands, the Vedas had become a means of making a living. They were trading on the sacred lore. The yajnas on which they laid so much stress had become more and more ritualistic: the killing of animals as sacrifices and the drinking of the juice of the Soma creeper became part of the essential rites and the end was forgotten as the means became more elaborate. No one paid any heed to salvation which should have been the purpose of the yajnas. To resurrect man from this fall from grace, to shake him out of this mental and moral stupor, some drastic steps were imperative.

In the beginning Bhagavan Buddha caused a sensation by his attack on the elaborate ritualism which was prevalent.

But, sadly enough, in his intense devotion to the fight against the decadence of the Vedas, he lost sight of vedanta which is the very essence of the Vedas. He spoke of compassion towards all living beings and about renunciation, but he did not speak about the Atman.

Later came the invasion of the Sakas, the Hunas and the Yavanas; and the Vedas and their message were almost obliterated. Society was caught in an eddy of uncertainty, a future without a goal.

The situation was desperate. The vital task ahead of the Vedic scholars was the reestablishment of the Bhagavata dharma. Several attempts were made to achieve this end, the most remarkable of which was the work done by Vyasa. He infused new vitality into the Vedic way of life and he presented it in a fresh framework, clothing it in the stories of the Mahabharata and the Bhagavata. The intervention of Vyasa was timely since the eclipse of Dharma was only too apparent. The two new schools of thought, Buddhism and Jainism, had dragged society far away from the right path. The rise of the Bhagavata dharma steadied the tottering edifice of society. Because of the glory of the Mahabharata, the Bhagavata and the Gita, Dharma was firmly established.

In the spiritual revolution whose aim was the renascence of the path of Dharma according to the Vedas, the greatest credit goes to Adi Sankara, the apostle of the Advaita philosophy. Sankara was a seer with a giant intellect and he revealed to the world the incompleteness of Buddhism. Buddha advocated that man should abandon all worldly passions, possessions and emotions, concentrating on renunciation or sanyasa. He did not talk about the Atman and its relationship with the Paramatma. Sankara, on the other hand, belonged to a different school of thought. He was himself a sanyasi and his teaching was entirely centered on the realization of the Brahman, on identifying the Atman with the Paramatma.

Caught in the magic web of Maya, man becomes a victim of delusion. In his ignorance he thinks that the "I" in him concerns only his body, mind, and intellect, which function at different levels, in different planes. He does not realize that these three are manifestations of the Atman in him which is the real cause of his entire being, his actions, his emotions, his thinking. Because of this ignorance of the real truth about the Atman he becomes involved in the cycle of births and deaths. Unless and until he rids himself of this delusion, this ignorance, man continues to wallow in the bondage of the world, the cycle of births and deaths.

This is, in short, the teaching of Sankara. It is clear from the many stotras he has composed that Sankara recommended the path of Bhakti also. It may appear he did not attach much importance to Karma yoga, but that is not so. In the four quarters of our country he established four Vidya Peethas and this is not possible for one who does not advocate Karma yoga.

Sankara, the great teacher, came after Buddha, and we are yet to see another man of such intellectual stature. He made such an impact on the minds of thinking men that the lesson he taught and the spiritual revolution he caused have left a permanent mark on this home of ancient culture. It is the opinion of some that the teachings of Adi Sankara had leanings more towards Nivritti marga (detachment), that he was not so emphatic about Karma, the performance of one's duties. But this is a wrong impression and there is no justification for it.

After Sankara came Ramanuja and he was followed by several great acharyas, Madhva, Vallabha, Nimbarka. All of them propagated the Bhagavata dharma. They taught men the path of Bhakti and all of them had a great leaning towards Nivritti marga. Many bhaktas appeared after these seers. In the South were the Alvars, Chaitanya in the North, and in Maharashtra, Jnaneshvar, Sant Tukaram, Samarth Ramadas and others. To this list of devotees belong the names of Surdas, Kabir, Nanak, Narsi Mehta, Mira, Dadu, Raidas. These are some of the many bhaktas who appeared as recently as within the last five or six hundred years. Each in his own way lightened the darkness around the world.

In those days, as we know only too well, the means of communication were very poor. Newspapers were unknown. In spite of this, bhaktas were able to spread their message of hope to all the four quarters. It seems like a miracle wrought by the Lord Himself.

The most common method was what is known as "Tirtha Yatra". During their wanderings from one holy spot to another the holy men conveyed to the people the cult of Bhakti. Bhajans were the predominant means of teaching. The bhakta had a troupe of followers with him and they would raise their voices together and sing bhajans in praise of the Lord. The village folk, drawn to them, would join in the singing and thus would the days and nights be spent. Music was greatly used to spread the lesson of Bhakti to people.

The language in which these songs were composed was simple; words were strung together in melodic rhymes. They were popular and could be learned easily. And so the lesson was passed on from mouth to mouth. The method was simple but the results were spectacular.

The heritage left by Krishna and other great thinkers was thus guarded and, later, propagated. This was entirely due to the efforts of the bhaktas and their bhajans. The peculiar feature of these bhajans is the homely, uncomplicated manner in which the highest truths of the Vedanta were expounded. Men learned these lessons without being aware of it. Their minds were filled with Bhakti and Vedanta too, indirectly, because of the bhajans. Nowhere else in history can one find an instance equal to the religious revival through bhajan.

When we study these songs composed by the bhaktas, when we think of the lesson they taught, it is evident that they speak mostly of Bhakti and the Nivritti marga. At the same time they do not lose sight of the Bhagavata dharma. They combine the two yogas, Bhakti and Karma, and the effect on the minds of men has been permanent.

A significant fact in the Bhagavata is the acceptance by Vyasa of Buddha as an avatara of Narayana. Vrishabha has also been said to be an avatara. Vyasa has thus averted the unpleasant controversies that were likely to arise between different schools of thought. This was indeed a great service he has rendered to India.

As a result of the combined efforts of great dedicated men, this ancient Dharma is very much alive and popular even after thousands of years. The culture of our land is mighty because of this basic Dharma underlying it. It is my desire to understand these original poems and to grasp the significance of the many paths by which this Dharma has been followed.

The Bhagavata is the storehouse of this Dharma. It abounds in stories of the many bhaktas of the Lord and the wondrous stories of Krishna. When he wrote the poem, Vyasa had in view the state of the society then and the threat of extinction which Dharma was facing. He wanted to instill Bhakti in the minds of men whose awareness of it was fast disappearing. He desired to lead them in the path of Karma, to make them realize their duties. To attract them he beautified his poem with myriads of charming stories and incidents from the life of Krishna, reading which they would surely be eager to tread the right path.

Yoga and Viyoga

The Gita tells of four different types of men. All of them are bhaktas but the approach of each is different. They are Artha, Artharthi, Jijnasu and Jnani.

Most men are either Arthas or Artharthis. When he is in great distress man turns to the Lord for help. This is an Artha. Else, he has a desire and he appeals to the Lord to help him achieve it. Again, if he has possessions he asks the Lord to help him keep them. This is the Artharthi. Man is so pathetic in his helplessness that the Lord, in His infinite mercy, looks kindly on him. Even if the desire in the heart of man is small, negligible, it has prompted him to call upon the Lord and this gesture on his part is enough to bless him.

In the Bhagavata the words spoken by Kunti are sublime. She says: "Krishna, whenever we were in trouble we thought only of you and every time you have responded to our call at once. Grant me this, my Lord. Let misfortune after misfortune visit us so that you will never be out of our minds and thoughts."

Once Krishna came to the forest when the Pandavas were there. Draupadi asked him: "Krishna, when the sinful Kauravas were bent on insulting me, when I stood helpless there in that court where no one had the courage to defend me and my honor, you saved me. But tell me, why did you not come earlier to my rescue and spare me the indignity to which I was exposed?" Krishna replied: "Draupadi, the fault was entirely yours. In the beginning you put your trust in your husbands and in your old grandsire Bheeshma, hoping that they would shield you. You did not think of me then. In the end, when everyone else failed you, you thought of me and, quicker than thought, I was there to help you."

The Artha is devoted to the Lord and his pathway is bhakti. But the Jnani is very rare to find, and perhaps one in a million is a Jijnasu, a Jnani. It stands to reason that the ignorant man—ignorant since he is steeped in Avidya—cannot be led towards the path of bhakti unless he is promised some kind of a reward! This is the truth behind the enticing words and incidents which are found in the Bhagavata, and in the other Puranas. Bhakti does, ultimately, rid man of his worldliness and draws him toward the path of Jnana; only, the process is gradual.

Vyasa has deliberately exaggerated the many descriptions in the poem. As was said before, his desire was to lead men towards the right path and he sought to make his method as attractive as he could. An example is the story of Ajamila, a confirmed sinner. His son's name was Narayana and when he was dying he called his son. And at once the attendants of Lord Narayana were by his side and they chased away the messengers of Yama. This incident is absolutely beyond the pale of logic, but Vyasa used such stories to serve his purpose, which was the welfare of mankind. The story is used to drive home the lesson that the Lord will ever respond to the call of the bhakta. This thought *had* to be instilled in the minds of men. If we can understand and grasp the secret of his writing, there is then no need to speculate on the strangeness of some of the stories.

However, a word of warning has to be spoken in this context. It should be remembered that the Bhagavata is not just a compilation of strange, unnatural events or stories. If one studies the book carefully it will be clearly evident that it is a great book, which is nothing else but a treatise on the Bhakti yoga, and the Bhagavata dharma. Like the Gita, this poem also gives us a happy blending of Bhakti and Karma yogas and draws the mind of the reader towards the contemplation of the Atman. It is only when one goes to the very depth of the teachings here that the truth is seen that the

Bhagavata is a commentary on Vedanta. In between the stories of bhaktas are interspersed dissertations on Vedanta, Karma and Jnana. This method is very effective. While reading about the life of the bhakta the reader is made to learn the more enduring lessons of Vedanta.

Let us take, for example, the conversation between Devahuti and Kapila Vasudeva. Devahuti was the daughter of Svayambhu Manu and the wife of Kardama, the son of Brahma. Acharya Kapila Vasudeva was their son. After the birth of his son, Kardama went off to the forest to perform tapas. Kapila remained with his mother. Days passed. Devahuti was slowly learning the art of detachment. She knew too that her son was the avatara of the Lord. She went to him and said: "Child, I have lost all interest in the world around me. Please teach me how to shed this web of Maya which has entangled me. Lead me to the path of Freedom."

Kapila then taught her the great lesson which helped her to realize herself, one of the most profound passages in the Bhagavata. He said: "Mother, you want to break away from the bonds which have tied you down to this world. Mother, bondage is caused by the involvement in the world of senses. This bondage can be shed if you cultivate the company of the good. Because of this, your love for the Lord and your devotion to Him will increase. This will lead you to become detached from the objects of the senses and in course of time you will be able to realize the truth about the Atman.

"Atman is another name for Ishvara. There is no difference between the Atman lodged in you and the Paramatma. The Atman has no gunas to taint it. It is the same Atman which is found in all of us. The plurality of the world around us is just apparent and not real. It is the Purusha out of whom is manifested the Prakriti. Purusha has no duties to perform nor is He bound by anything. He is the Seer lodged in you and me. Ignorance causes delusion in the mind: the delusion is that Ishvara is something apart from the Atman.

"Think of the sun. When he is reflected on the surface of water, surely he is not drenched by it! Even so, the Atman or Paramatma is untouched by the many travails which the body passes through. Mother, rid yourself of the shackles imposed on you by the senses. Be devoted to the Lord. Pursue your tasks, your duties with no thought of return or reward. When fire is born of the Arani, the piece of wood is itself burnt by the fire that it has produced. Even so, bhakti towards the Lord and Karma with selflessness will destroy the Vasanas. Go back to your duties, mother. Be satisfied with what you have, considering it to be the gift of the Lord. Let the food you consume be clean and pure. Have compassion towards all living beings and soon, very soon, you will attain the Freedom you ask for."

Kapila Vasudeva taught the lesson that one should continue with his daily duties with the special observance that no reward should be expected. The teachings of Kapila are a perfect blending of all the three yogas, Karma, Bhakti and Jnana.

The stories of Dhruva and Ranti Deva also belong to this category. They make the reader conscious of the truth about the Atman, the Paramatma and their relationship.

If people are under the impression that the Bhagavata is just a recounting of the pranks of Krishna, the Rasa Leela and the Vastraharan of the gopis, the stealing of the butter from their houses and similar episodes, then they have not understood the purpose of the poet. If one were to study the poem in the proper manner, with a desire to know what these stories mean, then they will find the Vedanta which permeates it.

It must be realized that the many pranks of Krishna were all played during the days he spent in Brindavan. The Bhagavata tells us that Krishna's age was seven when he lifted the hill called Govardhana. According to the *Harivamsha*, his age was just seven when he killed Kamsa. The Rasa Kreeda and the Vastraharan of the gopi maidens are stories of his boyhood: the locale of all these incidents is Brindavan.

Myriads of poems have been composed about Radha. Innumerable popular songs tell us of the love of Krishna for Radha. But in the Bhagavata there is no mention of this romance. Nowhere do we find the name of Radha. One is astonished by the fact that the many songs in praise of Krishna have, as their theme, the Krishna of these days, the Krishna of Brindavan fame. "The darling child of Nanda", "Nandalala", are some of the familiar names of Krishna. Mira sings about Krishna as *Govardhana Giridhari*. Jayadeva's *Gita Govinda* is about the divine lovers, Krishna and Radha, and the entire scene is set in Brindavan and on the banks of the river Yamuna. Krishna and Brindavan are always spoken of together in these many songs of the bhaktas. The poets do not seem to have evinced any interest in Krishna after he left Brindavan. It seems as though he is forgotten!

Krishna shed his peacock feather, his flute, his love for stolen butter when he left Brindavan. It looks as though Nanda, Yashoda, his companions, the gopas and the gopis, the entire boyhood he spent in Brindavan, were all completely forgotten by Krishna from the moment he stepped into the chariot brought by Akrura. Brindavan and its associations were all things of the past and not once did he look back and pine for those days.

And yet, it remains a matter of wonder as to why the poets considered the life of Krishna in Gokula as the vital theme in their songs of devotion. It still remains a mystery.

After the killing of Kamsa, Krishna's father Vasudeva performed the rite necessary for him to be pronounced a kshatriya. Great was the rejoicing in Mathura. The father then sent the brothers Balarama and Krishna to the gurukula of Sandipani and they were taught the sacred lore. Krishna was now well-versed in the Vedas and the Vedangas. As for the life among the gopalas, the entire chapter was, to him, a forgotten factor from the moment he set foot in Mathura. A new chapter had begun. Krishna is no longer a cowherd but a kshatriya. It looks as though the curtain falls on the previous act. Vraja Bhoomi is lost in the gulf of oblivion.

Many years later, there were assembled in Kurukshetra men, women, kings and princes. The occasion was the eclipse of the sun. It was almost like a pilgrimage for those who had come to the holy spot. Rishis of the earth, and the heavens too, were there. Kunti had come with her five sons and all the Kaurava clan.

Nandy, Yashoda and all the people from Brindavan had come to Kurukshetra. Their joy knew no bounds when they knew that their beloved Krishna was there. After a long lapse of time they met him. The meeting was an attempt to revive the past. Old memories came back bringing with them shades of happiness and of pain, as renewing what is past is neither possible nor is it completely pleasant.

But Krishna was lukewarm in his response. He had pushed those days away from him long ago and he could not share the emotion of the gopis. He told them: "My dear friends, ever since I left Gokula, I have become involved in many situations which prevented me from coming back to you. I am sorely distressed by it . . ." He spoke to them with great affection and concern. The gopis rebuked him a little for his indifference, but Krishna could not go back to the days of long ago. The women were not able to rekindle in him the old love which was once part of him. The past and remembrances of the past could not touch him.

He spoke to the gopis and his voice was grave. There was no mischievous smile on his face when he said: "Friends, meetings and partings are all preordained. The Lord brings them about. He is the sole cause of happiness and peace. This physical body is but an illusion. The Atman which dwells in the body is the only truth. That is eternal and cannot be destroyed. Remember this one fact. One Atman resides in all the many human beings. The Atman in you and Paramatma are but one. If you can grasp this truth there will be an end to your sorrow at the thought of the separation from me. There will then be no joy at the meeting of two beings nor will there be any sorrow when they are parted. Since the same Atman resides in both, where is the question of separation? The ultimate aim is to realize this truth. Why do you grieve that you are away from me? You and I are one."

The gopis were able to forget the past because of the words spoken by him. Krishna spoke words steeped in Vedanta and never once did he refer to the incidents which bound them together. To him they did not exist any longer. The days of his boyhood in Brindavan were now forgotten.

The Search for Truth

The purpose of the life of Krishna was to lessen the burden which was oppressing Mother Earth. He was born to destroy the wicked and to protect the Sadhus, the good and the gentle: to establish again the Dharma which was in danger of being forgotten. When the might of those in power increases, it follows that this power is misused, the weak and helpless are harassed. This sinfulness becomes a burden which the Earth is not able to bear. The savior of the people is said to lighten this burden.

Rama was born in the Treta yuga to put an end to the atrocities perpetrated by Ravana. In the Dwapara yuga, Kamsa Jarasandha, Shishupala, Dusshasana, Sakuni, Duryodhana and several others were sinful by nature and they had to be punished. Krishna's entire life was spent in bringing about their end. With the end of the tyrant tyranny also ends. However there was one unavoidable tragedy during this destruction of the evil-doers. Good men like Bheeshma, Drona and Karna were destined to be killed because of their siding with sinners. There was no doubt about their greatness but they had to die because of their association with sin.

Bheeshma and Drona, and to an extent even Karna, were waiting for their end. They were not happy. The thoughts and sympathies of the two old men were with the Pandavas, but they owed a debt of gratitude to Duryodhana and physically they belonged to him. During the war which they fought, this mental unrest made them desire death which could release them from their bondage and their divided loyalties. And this willingness on their part made the task of Krishna easier. To the end Karna was loyal to Duryodhana but the eagerness with which he prepared himself for the war disappeared when he learned that the Pandavas were his brothers. He was also ready to die and he welcomed death. The great war was fought and it brought about the end of the lusty kshatriyas. The burden of the Earth was lightened by Krishna.

The Mahabharata is unique in every way. In his own inimitable manner Vyasa has brought home to us the truth that sin and sinfulness are certain to be destroyed and even good souls if they associate with these.

But Krishna's task was not complete. In Dwaraka the Yadavas were vying with each other in strength and might. The youths were undisciplined and their arrogance was unbearable. Drinking was also responsible for their becoming blind to the difference between right and wrong. Tyranny became second nature to the scions of the royal house.

Krishna knew what was happening. The Yadavas had to be destroyed and this was possible only if they could be made to fight among themselves. No outsider could kill even one of the Yadavas. This was a privilege granted to the Yadavas and Krishna knew it only too well.

Soon the moment came for which Krishna was waiting. A drunken orgy sparked a small argument between two of them and soon this argument became a fight. The entire clan took part in the confused fight and in a short while they were all dead—all but Krishna, who stood apart and watched the death of his kinsmen. There was a look of sheer relief on his face as he was now free to leave the earth. His mission was now fulfilled and there was nothing left for him to accomplish. The purpose of his life had been served. He had but a few more days to live and he prepared himself for the departure. Uddhava, his companion, had realized earlier that Krishna would leave him soon and he went to Krishna with pain in his heart. Krishna comforted him and taught him the great lesson of Brahma Vidya:

Krishna said: "Uddhava, the time has come when I

should bid adieu to you. My days here on this earth are numbered. In another seven days this entire Yadava clan will be destroyed and Dwaraka will go under the sea. I suggest that you do not tarry here after my departure. Give up all attachments, teach yourself to look on the opposites with equanimity and spend the time on earth with your thoughts turned inwards. Uddhava, this world which is around you, which is filled with the objects of the senses, is false. It is not lasting. There is nothing permanent about it. The plurality whch you see is an illusion. Try to bring the senses under control and then you must try and realize that this entire universe is resting on Brahman and that your Atman is none other than this Brahman. Knowledge is knowing the essence of the Vedas: but the realization of the Brahman is Vijnana. Knowledge, that is jnana, leads to Vijnana. Once this truth is realized nothing can hurt or affect you."

Uddhava said: "It is not easy, Krishna, to do what you ask me to as I am greatly attached to beings around me."

Krishna then taught him in great detail the pathway of the approach to the truth. He told him: "You should continue with your daily duties. Shed attachment to the work you are doing and to the fruits of it; offer them all to me. Think of me and do your duty. Learn to control even your thoughts and set them on me alone. Yajnana and yagas promise the rewards of heaven, but you should pay no heed to them. These heavens are also not permanent. If it is not possible to control your thoughts, resort to the Bhakti marga and worship me. You will then find it easier to control your mind. Remember that the Atman in you is none other than the Paramatma and so be compassionate towards all living beings as the same Atman dwells in every one of them. You will soon be free of the bondage called Samsara. Bhakti, the easiest and the true path will soon grant you freedom."

Krishna spoke further about Atma Vidya and finally said: "Uddhava, proceed to Badarikasrama and persue this Tapas there." Uddhava took leave of him and went to Badari.

When dissertations like these are studied, it is clear the Bhagavata is not a mere narration of the pranks of Krishna. The relation of the Rasa Leela and such incidents is thus a sugar coating which has been laid on the serious lesson of the Bhagavata, to make it attractive and alluring.

The Name of the Lord

Literature should be pleasing, interesting and, at the same time, truthful. Vyasa's works had all these requirements. His poems, the Mahabharata and the Bhagavata, are both extremely pleasing. The stories are beautiful and interesting. In recounting them Vyasa has managed to make us familiar with the elements of the wisdom of the Vedanta which are woven into the stories. Because of this infusion of Vedanta, mankind becomes interested in the Bhakti and Karma yogas which he deals with. Study of these poems make men think along the right lines and they are persuaded to follow the path which leads to the knowledge of the Paramatma. Those who are eager to pursue Truth in the intellectual sphere are able to ignore the improbabilities in the stories which have been narrated. And, like gathering gold from the earth, they try to glean the grains of truth hidden in these stories. The poet has set the poem before the reader and he is welcome to choose whichever part he likes and get pleasure out of it. It is very much like a meal set before one, made up of dishes of different types. All of them are tasty and all of them are good. The guest chooses a dish and benefits by it. Even so are the poems of Vyasa. The reader can glance at the entire Bhagavata and choose what he likes and enjoy it to the full.

I wish to make one observation here. It is evident from the study of these two poems that Krishna of the Bhagavata is to be worshipped since he is endowed with qualities which are divine. Krishna of the Bhagavata is for the bhakta. It is not possible to emulate him since he is divine and who can follow the path trodden by a god? Krishna is Narayana Himself and he cannot be imitated. It is only possible to worship Him.

But Krishna of the Mahabharata is different. He is worthy of worship, too, but even more he is an example to be followed. The life of Krishna as presented in the Mahabharata is of great help to us when we are faced with difficult problems in life. In the Gita, Krishna himself has told us that everyone should follow him and his way.

This Krishna is a great character, well-versed in the nuances of Dharma. He has been called "Yogeshvara", "Buddha", "Dheera", "Kavi", "Prajna", "Pandita". His wisdom is accepted by everyone as the terms Buddha, Prajna and Pandita show. Kavi was the name given to Sukracharya for his wisdom and the name suits Krishna for excellent reasons. Krishna is a great figure in the Mahabharata. His life and his teachings have served as beacons to those groping in the wilderness of life. If one is able to understand the teachings of this great man and to follow them, then the most difficult and painful situations in life will cease to be so. Life becomes easy for one who has understood the life of this fascinating person.

Karma Kanda, as it was called, was then in the hands of the priests. This was part of the Vedas, but in the hands of the priests it had assumed an aspect entirely different from the one Vyasa had shown. Sacrificing animals and drinking the juice of the Soma creeper soon became very attractive to the priests and the real purpose of the yajnas, *nishkama karma*, was lost sight of. Along with the ascendancy of the priests there came into force the teachings of the Sankhyas which advocated Sanyasa. To rescue humanity from both these paths Krishna established the Bhagavata dharma. This Dharma, as has already been said, is a happy blending of the Bhakti and Karma yogas and it is the keynote of the Bhagavad Gita as taught by Krishna.

The word "Yoga" has been described very clearly by Krishna. He says: "Arjuna, what I am talking about is not new. This Karma Yoga has been there since ancient times. If I do not follow this Yoga, if I do not show interest in the performing of my duties, it will be wrong. People will follow me in what I do and for their benefit I will have to be engaged in work. In the three worlds there is nothing which I am compelled to do. I have no duty to perform. There is nothing which I desire, nothing which I have to strive for. And yet, I keep on with the pursuit of Karma. This is the reason for it. If I turn my face away from Karma, then people who emulate me will also avoid their duties and the results of that will be disastrous; society will fall to pieces if everyone shirks his duty. And, so, it is essential that you should do your duty.

"But then there ia a difference between the manner in which an ordinary man performs his duties and the path which I suggest. He is involved in the results of his actions. He is not detached. I suggest that, like him, you should also pursue your actions diligently. Only self-interest should be absent. The wise man has no thought for the results or rewards of his actions and with this detachment he works in the world of men. I have no desire for the rewards and those who have understood my words should do as I do."

The Lord has thus said clearly that He is an example to be followed. It should be borne in mind that Krishna of the Mahabharata should be followed and not Krishna of the other poem, the Bhagavata.

Krishna spoke: "In ancient times I taught this yoga to Vivasvan. He handed it down to Manu and Manu taught this lesson to Ikshvaku. This tradition has persisted through the ages. But now, at the present moment, it seems to have been forgotten. I am only recounting this age-old yoga to you since you are my friend and my bhakta."

It should be observed here that Krishna calls Arjuna his friend. He does not address Arjuna as though he were an incarnation of the Lord talking to his bhakta. The talk is as that between two friends and nothing more. Neither had Arjuna ever considered Krishna as an avatara of the Lord. He listens to him as he would to the words of a dear friend who is trying to help him out of a predicament. In the entire epic it is evident that the relationship between Krishna and the Pandavas is that of family kinship and their behavior towards him is that of ordinary cousins. Krishna was more than a cousin to them in their affection for him, but that was all. He was their friend and mentor and when they were in trouble, he was there by their side to assist them, to advise them on the course of action to be taken and to give them all the help he could. He had made the Pandavas promise that they would call him when they needed him and that they would never have any hesitation to do so. Never once did Krishna behave towards them as the Lord, the Yogeshvara. His divinity was concealed in the guise of a friend. This difference between the two Krishnas should be noted as it is a great difference.

Be that as it may, whether it is Krishna from the Bhagavata or the Mahabharata, the fact remains that he is worthy of worship for those who pursue the Bhakti marga. The names of Rama and Krishna have been, for ages, the means to attain Moksha. Krishna has said that his example should be followed for he was behaving like an ordinary being. But no one had paid much attention to these words of Krishna. The path suggested by him was by no means easy, and it was much easier to worship him as a god. This is the reason why Krishna of the Mahabharata has also been considered as the Lord Himself and worshiped.

It will not be quite right if we ignore the life of Krishna completely and remember only his name as the object of worship. Without Karma yoga, Bhakti alone is fruitless; and Karma yoga when it is not accompanied by Bhakti is again of little use.

The wonder of wonders is the fact that no one questions the veracity of the lives of Rama or Krishna. No one has been troubled, for instance, by the Rasa Kreeda of Krishna; no one is puzzled by the five chapters in the Bhagavata where this has been elaborated. The bhakta has no desire to talk about the episode. The bhaktas are certain in their minds that Krishna was Bhagavan Narayana Himself and that was enough for them. Narsi Mehta says that everything else is false and only Krishna is true; so say Tukaram, Mira and the other bhaktas. With the help of the Name of the Lord, by repeating it, it is possible to cross the ocean of births and deaths. It was so in the past and it will be so for ages to come.

This absolute faith in the Name of the Lord is a wondrous thing. It is well-nigh a miracle. When the time for leaving the world is fast approaching, the name of Rama should be spoken. This was the aim of the bhaktas and Gandhiji did utter the words, "Ram! Ram!" when he died. Gandhiji was a great bhakta and a Karma yogi, too.

The Lord has said: "Whenever there is dearth of Dharma, I will reincarnate myself as a human being. I will assume a name and a form to establish Dharma once again." The meaning is: when the edifice of society seems to tremble at the foundation, when there is danger of its deterioration, there is sure to be born some great soul, some great personage, someone endowed with unusual qualities whose appearance will rescue Dharma from the backsliding.

Krishna was one such personality and after him came Buddha. He was followed by Adi Sankara and then came other great teachers and bhaktas. In our times a divine light in the form of Gandhiji had appeared in our midst and he lifted Dharma from the depths to which it had fallen.

Realization

Rama and Krishna were considered to be avataras of the Lord. But then, in the Vedantic sense, every man is an avatara of the Lord as the same Atman resides in every one of us. Every being in this world is born for a purpose. He may not know it, but the Lord knows. He uses them as instruments for the tasks for which they have been born. Krishna tells Arjuna: "I have already done all that has to be done. I have decided the fates of all the men who have assembled here. You should be but the 'Nimitta', the instrument for me. I will take care of the rest."

There is a story prevalent that Krishna is the complete avatara of the Lord, with all the sixteen *Kalas* as they are called. When Rama was born, he had, at the beginning, only twelve *Kalas* of the Lord. After his wedding with Sita, when they were returning to Ayodhya, there was an encounter between Rama and Parasurama, the Bhargava. Parasurama was vanquished and, as he went away, four *Kalas* of the Lord which were with him became Rama's and he was a complete avatara after that. Having lost his glory, Parasurama went off to the forests to perform Tapas.

These interesting stories have an inner meaning. One is made to realize that every human being is, to an extent, possessed of the spark of divinity. It may be just a single *Kala* or a fraction of it, or it may be all the sixteen *Kalas*, as in the case of Krishna. Every man is born for a purpose and when he has served the purpose for which he is born, he goes back to where he came from. There is no plurality in our concept of the the Parabrahman. There is but one and this One is all-pervading. It appears to be manifested as many forms and many beings. The plurality is apparent and not real. The Paramatma is indivisible and the functioning of this entire universe is contained in this one Truth.

The Gita says:

ब्रह्मार्पणम् ब्रह्महर्विब्रह्माग्निः ब्रह्मणाहुतम् ।
ब्रह्मैवतेन गन्तव्यं ब्रह्मकर्म समाधिना ।।

The Karma which is dedicated to the Brahman is the Brahman. The means to this dedication is again Brahman. The fire in which the offering is made and the offering itself are again but the Brahman and so is the person performing the sacrifice. If one were to pursue the analogy further, this paper, this pen and ink with which this is bring written, and the writer too, are Brahman.

In the course of his talk, in the chapter where he describes his Vibhutis and his glories, Krishna tries to teach the same lesson. This is what he means when he says: "Among the Pandavas, I am Arjuna and Krishna among the Yadavas. Among the immovables I am the Himavan, Ganga among the rivers and among the lakes, I am the sea, the greatest of them all. I am the cunning in the mind of the gambler and among the fish I am the shark." To be brief, this entire universe is permeated by one Brahman. There is nothing here apart from It nor is there anything ELSE than the Brahman. So, it will be clear as crystal that there is nothing which is not the Brahman. The word avatara becomes meaningless as the Lord and his bhaktas are but the same.

This may be evident to the enlightened few, but they are really very few. It is not possible to worship the Absolute Truth which has neither a form nor a name. To comprehend it with the help of the senses is not possible. This is why Krishna tells us: "It is hard to worship the Absolute Truth. It is unmanifest. This is why worshippers have given a form to the object of worship and they find it easy to concentrate on this form." Krishna says that an avatara is a concrete representation of the Paramatma and worshipping it leads the bhakta to attain Nirvana gradually.

Krishna says: "Bheeshma, Drona, Jayadratha and all the others have already been killed by me. You need not worry about the rightness of your fighting them. Your duty is just to fight. Enter the field and victory is yours." These words should not be taken literally: that Krishna fought with each and every one of those mentioned and killed them. He had said that he would be born in the world of men when Dharma was in eclipse and when sin was rampant in the minds of men. When he said, "I will be born," it does not mean the son of Devaki but the Paramatma. We should understand that Krishna is the representative of that Paramatma. Even these words should be considered well. It seems strange that the Lord should take the trouble of being born into the world for the sole purpose of destroying evil. Surely it is not a great thing for him to destroy anything He pleases at will. The entire universe obeys the laws set in motion by Him and when the law is transgressed He can punish the wrongdoer at once.

What we are to understand is this: when the chain of causation finds its limit in one direction there will emerge, in the natural course of events, an occurrence which will force things to swing in the opposite direction. Sin will be counteracted by some event which will nullify the effect and reestablish Dharma. The power which will destroy sin will make its appearance. This is the Law of Nature and it will be followed as a natural sequel. Krishna means this when he says that he will create himself. He does not have to assume any particular form to destroy evil. He will set in motion the law of nature and the end will be achieved.

When, during the summertime, the sun sheds his scorching rays on the world it seems as though the heavens are raining fire. The rainy season is designed to counteract the effect of this heat. This is again because of the laws laid down by the Lord. It is not necessary for the Lord to issue orders for the rainy season to commence. Even so, when Evil is on the increase, some force, some other power will eventuate which will be able to control this evil and Dharma will regain the place it has lost. The cycle of appearance and disappearance will proceed on its own accord without the aid of any extraneous interference.

When Krishna speaks of his teaching this lesson of Karma yoga to Vivasvan it is obvious that he does not mean Krishna the friend of Arjuna, but the Paramatma.

Arjuna asks him: "What you say does not seem to be possible. They were all men of the long ago. Vivasvan and the others were living long before you were born and they do not exist now. You could not have known them. How then could you have taught this lesson to them?"

Krishna clarifies his statement and says: "You and I have been born innumerable number of times before now. Several births have we taken before we were born as Krishna and Arjuna. You are not aware of this, but I know about them." The meaning is obvious, if one thinks on it. The Paramatma was always there, is ever there and will always be there. This same Paramatma takes it upon Itself as a duty to assume a human form for the fulfillment of some particular task. Once it is completed there is no need for the Paramatma to remain here any longer and It is free to return to where It came from. This has happened earlier and again, in the future, when the need arises, it will happen.

One who knows the Brahman is himself the Brahman. Krishna was a Brahmavid, Knower of the Brahman, and so he was the Brahman. If and when you and I realize the Brahman, we will become Brahman and we will also be able to speak the same language which Krishna speaks! After the realization of the Brahman there is no doubt that we will all be avataras like Krishna.

BUT, unless and until this realization comes, the world of plurality does exist and we cannot think of the Atman in us as the Paramatma. We have understood the logic of it, but understanding is different from realization.

Swami Chinmayanandaji once gave a novel interpretation of the different types of men. He said: "It is true that all are avataras of the Lord. But the man who is full of Tamas, inertia, is enveloped in Maya and the animal in him is predominant. The one who has Rajoguna, active attributes, prevailing is a human being with human qualities. But the one who has sattvic, truthful, qualities in him will be a man with

divine attributes. Such a man who has qualities which are divine is considered an avatara of the Lord, whether it be Krishna or any other man endowed with sattvic qualities in him."

When he contemplates on the Gita, Vyasa salutes it in his mind and says: "I salute Krishna, preceptor to the world." Sanjaya calls Krishna "Yogeshvara" because he has realized Brahman. Krishna deserves these attributes. In spite of the human form he had donned for the welfare of humanity, Krishna was Parabrahman. He had a right to say: "I am the Brahman," because he was. He had become one with the Brahman. As long as one does not experience this he says: "Namah Shivaya" and once the realization comes that he is the Brahman the bhakta can say: "Shivoham". Those who have experienced it are able to say with certainty, "I am Brahman."

When we are able to see and perceive the singleness beyond the plurality, when we are able to see that this entire universe is but the one Brahman, then the words of Krishna can be repeated by us too: "I am Himavan among the immovables, the shark among the fish and the Ashvattha among trees."

There is no need for words once this state is reached. We are no different from Krishna nor is he anyone other than the Brahman. This feeling will be apparent only when the realization comes. The seen and the unseen are the same. The wave of the sea is no different from the sea. It is part of it. It is born in the sea, exists in the sea and is finally lost in the sea. The wave, while it is existing, may say: "I am the sea." Gold is gold whether it is in the form of a jewel or an ingot. When the oneness in the plurality is clear, then is the Brahman said to have been realized and one becomes the Paramatma, Ishvara, Brahman.

An Avatara Has a Cause

Narayana and Nara were rishis who were born again as Krishna and Arjuna. The purpose of their birth was one, and once it was served they abandoned the earth and went back to their heavenly abode. There is an interesting incident in the Mahabharata to illustrate this.

The war was over and the field of Kurukshetra was strewn with the bodies of the dead. It was an ancient custom that the victors in a war should occupy the camp of the vanquished and spend a night there. In accordance with this custom the victorious Pandavas led by Krishna entered the enemy camp. Bugles and conches announced their victorious entry.

After they had all arrived there, Krishna asked them to listen to his words. They stood before him silently waiting for him to speak. Krishna said: "Arjuna, take your Gandiva and your other weapons and descend from the chariot." Arjuna could not see why he was asked to do this. But he had always obeyed Krishna without asking why, and so he acted as he was bidden without speaking a single word. When he had taken up his weapons and his Gandiva, he descended from the chariot. Krishna then dropped the whip and the reins which had been in his hands for the last so many days and he also descended from the chariot. The moment Krishna abandoned it, Hanuman who was presiding over the banner flew into the sky and vanished from their sight. Even as they were watching in wonderment the chariot caught fire and in a matter of moments it was a heap of ashes. The Pandavas were stunned by this happening which they had not anticipated.

There were tears in the eyes of Arjuna. Ever since the burning of the Khandava forest this chariot was his and they had been inseparable. The chariot, the sound of whose approach would strike terror into the hearts of the enemies, was now burnt. Ignoring the tears in his eyes, Arjuna asked Krishna: "Krishna, what has happened? This chariot was given to me by Agni. It was with the help of this that I helped Agni to devour the Khandava forest. This was the chariot the approach of which was dreaded by the enemies, and now I see that it is but a handful of ashes. Tell me why has this happened?"

Krishna said: "Arjuna, this chariot has served its purpose. It has been the target of all the many astras and it withstood the fury of all those; even the Brahmastra could do nothing to it as I was seated in it. My presence prevented the astras from wielding their power over it. But now that is all over. You need this chariot no more and so I descended from it for the last time. The moment the purpose of the chariot had been served its end had come." Krishna continued: "Everything which has been created has a definite purpose. The moment the purpose is served, its destruction follows. This is true of human beings too. In this world of men, each one is born to achieve some particular goal. When that goal is reached, there is absolutely no need for him to remain. The world does not need him any more. It is true of you and me too. We have both been born into this world for a certain purpose. When that has been achieved we will both leave this world. We will have to remain here as long as there is something left for us to do. But the time will come when we have to go. That is yet to come; it is not yet time for us to leave the world."

This incident illustrates the lesson, the truth, that there is a purpose behind everything, behind the birth of every human being. Everything in this world has been created with a definite purpose behind it and it is but natural that it dies once this purpose is served. To understand the mystery of this, it will be necessary to elaborate on this theme. A casual comment will only confuse the mind of the reader.

An avatara has a purpose behind it: the establishment of Dharma, protection of the oppressed and the destruction of evil. This was why Krishna was born in the House of the Yadavas and he shed this human body once his mission was ended.

An avatara is the *Pratika* of Ishvara. By *Pratika* is meant an image, a symbol, something which will stand in place of the original. A stone image of the Lord is also a *Pratika.* As long as the breath of life does not touch it, the stone image remains a stone image. The feeling which prompts one to consider the image as representing the Lord Himself infuses the image with devotion. The image of the Lord becomes an avatara.

When a worshipper offers flowers and incense to the stone image he does it to the Lord who, according to him, is represented by the image and not just the stone image. Even so, when an avatara is recognized as such, when the godliness in the image is perceived, it is worshipped as the Lord Himself whose avatara it is. The worship is for Brahman whose avatara is the object worshipped. It is really immaterial whether the bhakta worships a stone image or an avatara; both represent the power that lies behind the universe, the power that creates, that sustains and that destroys it. With bhakti uppermost in his mind the worshipper imagines that the stone image is the Lord and accordingly worships it, and through it, Paramatma. This is the ultimate aim of the bhakta, to realize Brahman and the *Pratika* helps him in his quest for truth. The truth which is untainted by the three gunas is the power behind the universe and it has to be worshipped. The image represents the Brahman since the bhakta has infused divinity into it by the power of his imagination.

Krishna has said: "If a man is sincere enough, the image he worships becomes the god whom he worships. If, with sincere feelings, a man worships other gods, he does, in reality, worship only me, as I am the lord of all forms of prayers, Yajnas and poojas. Men are of different natures, different temperaments and in accordance with these they worship gods of different types. To me it is the sincerity and devotion that counts. I assure you that a man will be rewarded for his devotion to his chosen god. I will strengthen him in the bhakti and his devotion will, in reality, be rewarded by me. People of small intellect do not know my real nature. I am the unmanifest Truth, the Imperishable. But these small men think of me as a human being limited by the bonds which govern ordinary men. Even they will, in the end, reap the reward of worshipping the Lord."

The Power Behind the Image

There is, in the Mahabharata, the story of a Nishada youth whose name was Ekalavya. He was very eager to learn archery. With this desire in his heart he approached Drona, the Acharya of the Kaurava House. He went to him and beseeched him: "My lord, be gracious enough to teach me archery."

The Acharya asked him: "Who are you?"

The youth replied: "I am the son of the king of the Nishadas."

Drona said: "You are not a Kshatriya and I will not teach you archery."

The youth went away from his presence, but he was not ready to admit his disappointment. He went back to the forest. He fashioned an image of Drona out of clay and installed it in his home. He considered it as his guru. With this in mind, the young Nishada began to learn archery. His sincerity and his concentration made him practice archery and soon he was an expert in the art of using the bow and arrow. He had gained mastery in the art.

Once the Pandava youths went to the forest. They had a dog with them which wandered into the forest. When it saw the Nishadha, it began to bark at him. Ekalavya took up his bow and arrow and shot at the dog. He did not want to kill it nor did he wish to hurt it. He made a network of the arrows and they were so skillfully placed on the muzzle of the dog that it could not open its mouth and bark.

The dog rushed back to the Pandavas. When they saw this strange sight they were amazed. Never once had they seen such skill with arrows and they rushed to their Acharya and told him about it. They ended with the words: "You have taught us archery, but we have not this skill." While Drona was nettled by their words, his curiosity was kindled and he wanted to see the archer who could work such wonders with his arrows.

He went with the Pandavas to the forest and soon reached the spot where the young Nishada was living. He went to him and asked him: "Child, who taught you this mastery over archery?"

Ekalavya replied: "My preceptor is Dronacharya. I have learned at his feet."

Drona was astonished as he did not remember having accepted him as his pupil. After questioning him further it came to light that a clay image of the guru was able to work this wonder.

The incident illustrates the truth that sincerity and devotion are capable of working wonders. Because of them the power which is worshipped will enter the image which will therefore become a symbol of the divinity worshipped. The bhakta will realize his dreams because of this.

The worship of the Pitris, gods, guru, brahmin, an athithi (a guest to one's home), or a cow is paying homage to Bhagavan Narayana Himself. This is the greatness not of the image, itself, but of the divinity which is symbolized by it. The guru is to be worshipped as he is said to be an image of the Brahman and so are one's father and mother. The story of Dharma Vyadha tells us how the man, by profession a butcher, would work hard in his shop by day and in the evening worship his parents at home and how he ultimately became one with the Brahman as he was a perfect Karma yogi. His worship of the father and mother was, in reality, the worship of Brahman.

Again, Agni, the god of fire, has been considered as Ishvara and the Vedic hymns sing his glory: "Agni, lead us in the auspicious paths and help us to turn away from the wrong paths." All these stories are there to tell us that the worship of the image of the Lord, when performed with sincerity, faith and affection, will be worship of the Lord and the bhakta is rewarded.

In the Vedas it is said: "The Atman prays to itself for its well-being, kindles the goodness in itself and gets what it desires." The Upanishads speak this truth: "This entire universe is pervaded by Ishvara."

This entire universe is enveloped, permeated, pervaded by Ishvara. Therefore the one who prays and the one to whom the prayer is offered are one and the same.

Bhakti in the heart of the devotee is roused and this leads to the gradual weakening of the grip of the Vasanas, the passions. It leads man into paths which are noble. This is why the rishis have given a form and feature to the absolute Brahman. It is not possible to delve deep into the mystery of these happenings. We can only repeat the words from the Gita: "Ignorance throws its cloak over the wisdom of man and it is this ignorance which deludes him into thinking: 'I am a human being; I possess a body, a form and feature, and a name'."

Strangely enough, this "Moha", this delusion, is very necessary so long as we live in this world. It can be considered to be the first step towards one's ascent into the world of spirituality. This first step leads one to the heights and without it the journey cannot begin. For instance, the alphabet does not comprise the Vyakarana of Panini, but one has to master the alphabet before proceeding into the study of grammar. Only one should not halt on this first step but proceed further.

Bhakti yoga as well as Karma yoga end in Jnana yoga and become one with it. Jnana is the last step in this journey towards truth. But Moha is the first step.

Bhakti in the Vedic language is not the same as the Bhakti which an emotional devotee feels. Krishna says: "Those whose thoughts ever dwell on me, who worship me and are lost only in contemplating on me, who think of me with Bhakti, are dear to me. I will take care of their yoga and their welfare . . ."

Yoga is a joining together and here is meant the acceptance of the bhakta by the Lord. Kshema is the protection assured to the bhakta accepted by the Lord. One fact, however, should be borne in mind: the bhakta should let his thoughts dwell on the Lord constantly. His senses must be under perfect control and his worship should be continuous. Then and only then will the Lord look on him kindly and accept him.

The Lord is not something apart from us. He is lodged within us. To quote Nanak: "Like the perfume dwelling in the heart of the flower which has just opened its petals, Hari dwells within you. Search for him there, inside you."

Commentators have illustrated this truth by a homely example. Gold is wrought into ornaments of different shapes and sizes, but the gold in all of them is the same. There is no difference between the gold in a necklace and that in an earring. There is no difference between the sea and the waves playing on its surface. Even so, there is no difference between the Atman and the Paramatma. But this realization of the truth comes only at the end of the spiritual quest. It is not possible to say "Shivoham" at the beginning because the truth would not have been realized yet. The first step, then, is essential.

If one pursues this introspection with single-mindedness, if one's desire is to realize this oneness with the Paramatma, then Yoga, the joining, will be achieved. The Yoga which seemed to be beyond one's grasp is realized and when that happens, the state, the Brahmi state, will never be shaken. This is what is meant by Kshema.

It is a rule in life that certain events will logically follow certain actions. If we act in this world, do our duties without any selfishness tainting the actions, if we act, leaving the result in the hands of the Lord, if we act with faith, then, according to the law of nature, the results of the action will follow even if we do not strive for them. There is no partiality in the Laws of Nature.

The language of the Vedas cannot be understood by the ordinary minds. The brahman which is devoid of the three gunas, which is beyond the grasp of the intellect, is something the human mind cannot comprehend and so the Nirguna Brahma is invested with a form. Man is told that God assumes this human form for the sake of protecting Dharma. He should be worshipped if His grace is desired. If we wish that our Yogakshema should be borne by him, then it is necessary for us to change ourselves. We should become sadhus, meaning we should develop a good character, selflessness, a desire to help others, and we should have nothing but goodness in ourhearts. In short, worship the Lord with a desire for nothing and your welfare will be in His hands. In the language of the Vedas or the easier one of bhakti, the lesson is the same: without becoming a sadhu one cannot aspire to achieve what is beyond one's reach. Bhakti gains for man the divine heritage which is greater than all the wealth of the three worlds.

Realization of Brahman—Soul Experience

In the twelfth chapter of the Gita, Arjuna asks a vital question of Krishna. All through the previous chapters several doubts of Arjuna have been cleared by Krishna. He has described his Vibhutis, attributes, to Arjuna and later his Vishvarupa, the cosmic form of the Lord, was also revealed to Arjuna. Both the yogas, Karma and Bhakti, had been described in great detail. After all this, Arjuna's mind was still clouded with doubts. Perhaps the doubts arose only after he had heard the previous words of Krishna.

With great hesitancy Arjuna asks: "Krishna, you talk of two types of bhaktas. One is the Karma yogi who worships you by just doing his duty without thinking of the results. There is the other one who worships the absolute Truth which is beyond the grasp of thought, which has no form on which to contemplate. Tell me, Krishna, which of these two is the better path? Which is superior to the other?"

Krishna answered: "The one who sets his mind on me, his thoughts on me, and lets them dwell on me incessantly and, with his mind set on me, works in the world of men as a Karma yogi, is the better yogi. The other one, after bringing his senses under absolute control and with his mind set on doing good to everyone, contemplates on the Brahman. This brahman is permanent. It cannot be defined. It is not manifested. It is all-pervading. The mind cannot grasp It. It is immovable and It is the base on which rests this entire fabric of the universe. This bhakta contemplates on this Brahman and reaches me in the end. But the path he has chosen is hard and beset with many hardships. One who has a body and mind cannot conceive of a truth which is formless."

It is clear that the worship of an avatara has been defined as dear to the Lord. It is an easy path and it leads to the Ultimate Truth which the other worshipper seeks in the contemplation of the Brahman.

In the ninth chapter, the path of bhakti has been explained fully. Krishna says, "This is an easy path to follow and it is certain to lead the bhakta to the Lord. At the same time, it should be remembered that the bhakta who favors the image of the Lord, his avatara, in preference to the worship of the Brahman, should bear in mind that I am the Brahman which pervades the universe. The worship of Saguna Brahman, as it is termed, should be with the knowledge that this same is but the Nirguna Brahma. He should be aware of this truth. The object of worship is not so important; it can be an image of stone, an avatara or even a great human being. What is of vital importance is the method of worship. Faith, sincerity, devotion, dedication are the essentials in the bhakta. Such a bhakta will surely reap the reward which is the same as that meted out to the other devotee."

History tells us that any task which is undertaken with a view to do good to others, to the world in general, and which is performed with a clean and pure mind, will certainly be a success. This is an assurance given to the Karma yogi. Similarly, workship of the Lord with constant Bhakti will bring nothing but good to the bhakta. Bhakti is a field where faith reigns supreme and there is no need here for speculation or discussion.

The field in which the senses function is indeed extremely limited. The range of the mind and the intellect are greater than that of the mere Indriyas, but they are also limited. Beyond a certain limit these prove insufficient to scan the field where the Truth lies. With such limited equipment at our command it is not possible to try and grasp the truth about the Brahman, about something which is infinite, incomprehensible, and which is unmanifested. The only way to describe it is the negative method, meaning, it is not this and it is not that. If, however, one tries to say, "It is this" and says that he can define it, then it is just words spoken by one who is full of ego. It is not possible to define the indefinable and to describe what cannot be described. And this is why it is futile to explain the truth about *Pratikas* and avataras with arguments trying to prove their divinity. This only tends to shatter the faith of the bhakta and is harmful to him as he must begin his worship with implicit faith and sincerity. His chosen god needs no explanation—he needs to be worshipped. Faith and only faith will gain for him admission into the world of Bhakti, where there is no place for discussion.

In the Brihadaranyaka Upanishad there is a very intructive episode. The story is laid in the city of Videha. Janaka, the king, has made preparations for the performance of a yajna. Scholars from many countries, like Kuru and Panchala, have come to attend it. During one of the assemblies, Janaka decides to find out who is the greatest scholar among them. He has with him a thousand cows, their horns decked with gold, and he announces to the scholars: "Wise ones, the best among you is at liberty to lead these cows home."

Yagnavalkya, who is present, tells his disciple that he can lead the cows home. Naturally there are objections from the others and the discussions begin. The others are not prepared to accept the supremacy of Yagnavalkya. They say: "How can you be sure that you are the wisest among us all? There are so many here who are well-versed in the Vedas and the Vedangas." Ashvala, a scholar in the court of Janaka, speaks up: "Do you really consider yourself to be the wisest of us all?"

Yagnavalkya replies: "I prostrate before the wisest scholar on the face of the earth. But these cows do belong to me."

Ashvala then begins to ask questions to examine the mastery of his opponent in the shastras. Yagnavalkya replies suitably and the questioner is silenced. Others take up where Ashvala is forced to leave off and so it goes on. Yagnavalkya has an asnwer to every question. Finally it is the turn of

Gargi. She is a great scholar and well-versed in all the shastras. She asks questions of Yagnavalkya:

"We are all covered, enveloped by water. What covers the waters?"

"Air."

"And the air?"

"The sky."

"What covers the sky?"

"The world of the Gandharvas."

"What is beyond this world?"

"The world of the sun."

"And beyond that?"

"The region belonging to the moon."

"Beyond that?"

"Is the region of the stars."

"What then covers this region of the stars?"

"The land of the gods and that is enveloped by the world of Indra."

"And Indra loka?"

"By that of Prajapati."

"What is beyond that?"

"Brahma loka."

Gargi then asks: "What is beyond Brahma Loka?" Yagnavalkya says: "Gargi, you are transgressing the limits. If you dare to go beyond this, it is dangerous for you. What you are asking about is something beyond the comprehension of the intellect. Do not ask questions about these abstract subjects."

We are not interested in what the sequel of the discussion was. The purpose of this narration is to repeat the sentence spoken by Yagnavalkya: "You are treading on dangerous ground as you are trying to reach beyond the limits of the intellect."

Gitacharya has also declared this same truth. He said: "This world is full of mysteries. Only to the chosen few is it known and some of them say that it is a wonderful sight and others say that it is wonderful to talk about it. Even after listening to their words this secret of the universe is not possible to understand."

At the point where the intellect fails to proceed further, the field of faith begins. There is, at this point, a blank wall which cannot be scaled by arguments and discussions. The Truth cannot be revealed by the knowledge of it. It has to be realized and when it is realized one becomes the Brahman.

Karma Yoga in the Gita

Some scholars are of the opinion that the first six chapters of the Gita deal with Karma yoga, that the next six comprise the Bhakti yoga, and that the last six are devoted to Jnana yoga. Perhaps there is some truth in this but to the general reader of the Gita this division seems to be artificial.

The chapters in the Gita have all been given names. Each has a particular appellation after it. Accordingly, the third chapter of the Gita has been named "Karma yoga" and the twelfth chapter is "Bhakti yoga". But, to the reader of the Gita it is evident that these three yogas are so intermingled that in each chapter traces of all three of them can be found. The division may be apparent to the scholar but not to the casual reader.

Be that as it may, the question which is posed to us is: Is there much difference between the paths of Karma and Bhakti? Has Krishna placed more emphasis on Karma and Bhakti? Has Krishna placed more emphasis on Karma yoga than on the others and, if so, why? What is the definition of this Yoga? How is one to set about it? These are some of the questions that tease the reader when he thinks of Karma yoga.

There is the suggestion by Krishna that Yoga should be sometimes called "skill": "Yogah Karmasu Kaushalam." How is one to be skillful in the performance of one's duty? This is elaborated in the sloka: Yogasthah kuru karmani sangam tyaktva Dhananjaya Siddhaasiddhah samo bhutva samatvam yoga uchyate." "Samatva" is yoga, says the Lord. What does the word mean? What is the essence of Bhakti yoga and how is it different from Karma yoga? How is one to follow this yoga?

There are, in the Gita, three great descriptions. The first of them is that of the "Sthithaprajna". The second is the description of a bhakta. There is a third section where the one who is beyond the reach of the gunas has been described. What is the difference between these? Krishna has explained all these, answered these questions very clearly in a concise manner and his instructions are precise. Actually, the dissertations are so clear and easy to follow that one feels it will be good for the aspirant to know these words, memorize them so that they can be repeated at will.

The Gita is a portion of the Mahabharata and it is an important section of it. Vyasa has said that it is the very essence of the Upanishads. In the dhyana sloka of the Gita occurs the statement: "The sacred cow by name Gita is all the Upanishads put together. The Lord Himself is the one who has deigned to milk this cow. And why? To what purpose? To give the milk of it, the essence of the Upanishads, to those of good intellect, while Arjuna is the calf which makes the cow yield all this milk." Krishna has filled a cup of gold to the brim with this milk and he has offered it to those who desire freedom from the bondage of births and deaths. There are no conditions set here. Anyone who wants to can drink out of the cup and benefit by it. The thirst for knowledge impels the seeker to drink of the cup and the Lord is only too happy to offer it to him.

It must be observed here that there are repetitions in the Gita. But these repetitions are there because Vyasa has a purpose behind this. It is not possible to quaff the contents of a cup in a single mouthful. One should take sips of it and that is the only way in which one can enjoy it. This example will, perhaps, explain the frequent repetition of the same words in the Gita.

Since time immemorial the two paths, Nivritti and Pravritti, have existed and they have been followed. The teachers of the Nivritti marga have named it "Sankhya" and Pravritti marga goes by the name "Bhagavata dharma". In the Bhagavata dharma, Karma yoga and Bhakti yoga have been blended inextricably. Nor is the Bhagavata dharma new. It was in vogue in ancient times but with the passage of time there seems to have been a neglect of it and its importance was not appreciated. Sri Krishna is responsible for infusing this Dharma with new life.

This Dharma has been dealt with in the Mahabharata, the Bhagavata and the Gita. This has been an attempt on the part of the Lord Himself to lead wandering minds away from wrong paths which they were pursuing and to guide them along the proper paths. The Bhagavata dharma which had almost been forgotten was brought to life and this was taught with great emphasis to erring mankind. Man was told where his duty lay. Pravritti was the marga which was recommended. Karma yoga is the main feature of the Gita and the propagation of this was the sole aim of Krishna.

The great war on the field of Kurukshetra was about to begin. All the preparations had been completed. The quarters were resounding with the noise made by the clashing of steel. The warriors were filling the air with the deafening music of their conches and each was vying with the other in his eagerness to fight. The air was thick with their war cries.

It was then that Arjuna said: "Krishna, lead my chariot and place it between the two armies. I want to see the many heroes arrayed to fight against us in this war." Without speaking a word Krishna took up the reins in his hand and the whip in the other. He led the four white horses which were yoked to the chariot of Arjuna. He stationed the chariot between the two armies as desired by Arjuna and said: "Look, Arjuna. Look at this immense army of the Kauravas spread out before you. These are the people whom you have to fight."

Arjuna cast his eyes on all of them. Look where he would, he saw men who were all his kinsmen. He saw his grandfather (Bheeshma), his acharya (Drona), his friends, cousins, playmates of his boyhood days. looking at them and thinking on the impending war and bloodshed, Arjuna's heart was full of sorrow and compassion. His mind was bewildered and his feelings were all mixed up. He could not contemplate the death of all these at his hands. He said: "Krishna, I am feeling as though a fever is burning my body. My skin is parched and my Gandiva is slipping from my hands. It seems to me, victory gained at the cost of so may lives, the lives of all these who are near and dear to me, is no victory at all. I do not want to kill them. I would rather be weaponless and be killed by Duryodhana and the others. Death seems infinitely superior to this killing of my kinsmen."

He let the bow remain where it had fallen and sat silent. His face was a study in pain.

This weakness in Arjuna made Krishna feel sorry for him. With a slight smile, half pitying and half amused, Krishna said: "Arjuna, this weakness does not become you. This unnatural conduct will but lead you away from glory, from the heavens which should be earned by you. How did this weakness descend on you? You will only court infamy by this weakness. Abandon this attitude and get ready to fight."

His words could not rouse Arjuna from his apathy and he said: "My mind is completely confused because of my emotions. I will not fight." And Arjuna sat silent after these words.

Krishna's teachings begin from this moment when Arjuna said: "I will not fight." He begins his talk with an explanation of the truth that the Atman is indestructible. He resorts to the Sankhya yoga and explains to Arjuna the Nivritti marga. "This Atman is all-pervading," says Krishna. "It is eternal and immortal. There is no need here to talk about the killer, the killing and the killed."

In the Mundakopanishad is a sublime description of the Brahman. It says: "It is not to be seen. It is beyond the comprehension of the senses. It is never born. It is not endowed with the sense organs like the human body. The manifest world is because of the Brahman and it envelops this entire universe. It is extremely subtle and it is whole, entire, complete, and it cannot be divided into component parts. Out of it is manifested Prakriti, the entire world of living and nonliving things. The wise realize this Brahman which cannot be explained by mere words." This is the language which is used in the Upanishads to indicate the Brahman.

In the Gita there is but a repetition of the words spoken

in the Upanishads. Krishna continues: "Man sheds the garments which are old and takes up new ones. Even so, the Atman which dwells in the body abandons this body which has grown old and makes a new body its abode. There is no such thing as death as far as the Atman is concerned; and, consequently, no need to mourn the 'death' of anyone since no one dies. The Atman cannot be destroyed. This grief is the result of ignorance. It does not befit you since you are intelligent. This body was not there in the beginning nor will it last for ever. This makes its appearance during the course of the journey of the Atman. It is not permanent and no one should grieve for the end of the body. You are a wise man, Arjuna, but your words are those of an untutored, ignorant child."

When he sees that this talk on the Atman has no effect on Arjuna, Krishna says: "Let us forget the philosophical aspect of your problem. Even if we consider your conduct from the worldly point of view, it is to be condemned. The world will call you a coward. They will say that you turned your face away from the field of battle because you were afraid. Heroes will brand you with the infamous word 'coward' and this infamy will be hard to bear.

"I have explained to you that the Atman is indestructible and so you must not grieve for these men. I will alter my approach and tell you about Karma yoga, the path of Pravritti as against Nivritti. You will then realize the one important fact that if a man performs his duty with a sense of equanimity, with his mind perfectly poised, he will be rid of the bondage of Karma."

The core of the teachings of the Gita is Karma yoga and Krishna begins to dilate upon it in earnest from the thirty-sixth sloka of the next chapter. In the later chapters, Karma yoga and Bhakti yoga are dealt with together. Again and again they are dealt with, now separately, now together, and the features of each of these are explained in great detail. It follows, naturally, that there are several repetitions of the same lesson. The two paths terminate in the path of Jnana. They merge with this third path and freedom from this transient world is assured. This is the essence of the teachings of the Gita.

Again and again Krishna says: "Never should a man give

up action in the world." During those days, the days when the great war was fought, Karma Kanda was the most popular path advocated by the priests. Karma Kanda is different from Karma yoga and this is what Krishna is trying to instill in the minds of his listeners. The prevalent custom then was the performance of yagas or yajnas, which were said to grant the heavens to the yajamanas. The rites were elaborate and the sacrificing of animals and the drinking of Soma juice were part of the rituals. As time passed, the rituals gained supremacy over the spirit of the yajnas.

Krishna wanted to cure humanity of the delusion created by these rites which went by the name "Karma" and he succeeded in giving an entirely new meaning and interpretation to it. "Performing one's prescribed duties is Karma yoga," says Krishna. The Karma Kanda of the priests held out promises of the heavens. Krishna says: "If people pursue the pleasures of the senses and the gratification of them, if they are interested more in these passing pleasures than in what is good for them ultimately, they are ignorant. It is indeed sad that they are so much involved in the enjoyment of these pleasures that they perform these elaborate yajnas to get the assurance that these same pleasures will last forever, that in the heavens they can continue to indulge in them. But they are striving in vain. Neither will they have the steadiness of mind and purpose nor will they obtain peace or freedom from bondage. Freedom should be the aim of the seeker. And so, I tell you, forget all thoughts of the heavens and their transient pleasures which are promised by the Karma Kanda. Apply yourself diligently to the task ahead of you. Do your duty with the resolve that attachment to the results of your action should never color your action. There should be no desire for returns or rewards. Realize what your duty is, and pursue it. Man has the right only to act. The results are in the hands of the Lord. This is evident. If it is so, if the results of your actions are never in your hands but in the will of the Lord, what is the use of wasting one's thoughts on these? The thirst for rewards should be given up completely."

This type of teaching by Krishna was essential to the men at that time as Karma Kanda had gained ascendance and, along with it, Nivritti marga was popularized by some.

Between these two, Bhagavata dharma was ignored and there was a threat of it becoming forgotten altogether. People were becoming indifferent to Pravritti marga and it was necessary to infuse into the minds of men the lesson of selfless action and Pravritti as against Nivritti. That "man should act with a desire to do good to all living beings" was the teaching of Krishna from the beginning and this is the thread running unbroken throughout the Gita.

Wherever Karma is mentioned in the Gita it goes without saying that Krishna means action without attachment to the results, doing the duties assigned to one and bearing in mind the welfare of mankind. Krishna repeats this again and again and this is the basis of the teachings in the Gita.

In the beginning, Arjuna is overcome with sorrow at the thought of the painful task ahead of him and shirks doing his duty. As the discourse of Krishna proceeds, Arjuna asks different questions of Krishna which are answered with patience and affection. Krishna tells Arjuna about his Vibhutis and he reveals his Cosmic form also. He explains Jnana yoga too. Underlying all these is the emphasis on Karma yoga which flows like an unbroken stream throughout the entire discourse.

Karma and Sanyasa

In the beginning Arjuna had declared that he would not fight and Krishna said: "Do your duty. Do not take refuge in inaction." As has been mentioned before, this lesson is repeated by Krishna often. It is not so much repetition as an elaboration of a theme. It is like a skilled musician taking up a raga, singing it in many ways, in Alaps, and Taans and Swaras, each in its own way revealing the essence of the raga to the listeners; thus Krishna uses different words and situations to emphasize the lesson which he is trying to teach.

Sankhya was first dealt with; and the permanence of the Artman and the transient nature of the world around us was explained. Arjuna was confused as the talk proceeded along these lines and at a certain stage he asks: "Krishna, in the beginning you laid stress on Jnana and now you are asking me to involve myself in this cruel war as, according to you, it is a duty to be performed. I am confused. Tell me truly which is really good for me."

Krishna said: "Arjuna, as I told you, there are two ways of thinking prevalent in the world. Sankhya teaches Nivritti marga—Jnana yoga. And the other Yoga is Karma yoga. No man should abstain from the performance of Karma. He will not reap the reward of withdrawing from Karma even if he takes up Sanyasa. No man can exist, even for a moment, without action of some kind. It is the law of nature that man must act in some manner or other as long as he lives in this world. In reality, even if a man keeps his senses under control and prevents them from functioning, still his mind will be active and will be dwelling on the objects of the senses and so his 'control' of the senses is not genuine. However, if a man is able to control his mind, if he can dwell in the world of objects without getting involved in it as he has his mind reined in, if, in such a frame of mind, he can work in this same world for the welfare of mankind, such a man is said to be great. That is why I ask you to do your duty. Action is superior to inaction. Because, if one gives up work, it is not possible for him to continue to live. Do not succumb to inaction.

"Understand this: action which has been prompted by selfish motives, and which does not aim at the welfare of others, will surely involve you in bondage and you cannot be free of it. Such a man will fall further into the abyss of bondage. However, if the attitude is changed, if the desire is only the welfare of those in the world around you, then you are saved. Act accordingly, Arjuna. The Lord is Karma: consider it thus. Performing one's duty is service to the Lord. This wheel of Dharma is propelled by Karma alone. Give up all thoughts of self and proceed in this world of action. Never should one ignore the duties which have to be performed. Selflessness is the secret behind Karma yoga. Consider Janaka. He was a king and his duty was to rule his kingdom. He did his duty without any selfish motive and in the end he realized the Brahman. Service to the world can be achieved only by Karma yoga. If the good, the chosen few, refuse to do their duties the ordinary man will do likewise and that would be harmful to society. Tell me, is there any need for me to work? I have no duties incumbent on me. But, not even for a moment have I ignored my duties. If nature were to turn her face away from her duty, the entire universe will fall to pieces. The sun and moon will no longer move in their appointed orbits; the sea and the rivers, the very air and fire will refuse to do what they have been designated to do and what will be the state of this entire universe?

"What the ignorant man does with desire prompting him, the wise does sans desire. The ignorant man should not be asked to give up the work he is doing but he must be taught the proper method by which he should proceed: without selfishness.

"Nature makes the world dance at her behest. The ignorant man thinks 'I am going on with this task' while the wise man knows that everything in the universe proceeds according to the will of the Lord. When this truth is realized man will give up his attachment to the fruits of his actions.

"The ideal man is one who offers the results of his actions to me, worships me and continues to live in this world without any attachment to anything. This man will soon be rid of his Vasanas—lusts and attachments—and freedom from bondage will follow. For one who does not act thus, there is nothing in store but unhappoiness. Man, caught as he is in the world of action, will have to be doing something or other every moment. Nature, which is indeed extremely powerful, will drag him toward the world of the senses. How is one to prevent it? The way to overcome the sway of the senses is this: do not give up your actions. At the same time abandon the involvement in the opposites created by the senses: opposites like pleasure and pain, happiness and sorrow. Surrender the results of your actions to me and be indifferent to them. Thus should one act in the world. Desire and anger are the two powerful enemies of man. These two hold their sway over the mind of man. So great is their power that the intellect becomes clouded when they are in ascendancy. This is the reason why the Indriyas, senses, should be under perfect control. These two will then be held at bay and the Karma yogi will succeed in his selfless journey through life.

"The lesson I am teaching is not new by any means. It has been handed down through the ages by tradition. I have taught this to Vivasvan who handed it down to Manu and from Manu this came down to Ikshvaku. The sacred Bhagavata dharma has been lost in the mists of oblivion and it is this forgotten factor that I am recounting to you. Do what the ancients did and find the easy path to Moksha, Release.

"The study of Karma is not easy. What is action? What is inaction? What is wrong action? These are three things which should be studied and understood properly. The stories of Janaka and of Dharma Vyadha, who were Karma yogis, have been related already. Thuladhara was a Vaishya who pursued the craft of his birth in a detached manner.

"If one's duty is performed in the manner taught by me this same action becomes the equal of yajna as it is for the good of mankind. When the Lord created the universe he crated yajna along with it. He told man: this yajna is the Kamadhenu which will grant you all that you seek. Observe this yajna. Perform yajna so that the world will benefit by it. In return the world will think well of you and cherish you. When you perform yajna for the good of others then you will be granted favors even if you do not ask for them. Those who work only for themselves and for their selfish ends are like thieves who steal what belongs to others. The good will work for the welfare of others.

"Remember, doing just your duty is not enough. It should be accompanied by a mind with no selfishness. The periphery which restricts Karma is clearly defined. Action which is performed according to these rules can be considered a yajna. The rest is wrong action.

"There is a yardstick which measures Karma and the quality of Karma is determined by this. When a man, for instance, kills another, it is considered to be murder. If, however, this same man meets his death as a result of the judgment pronounced on him in a court of law, then his death does not lie at the judge's door. It is justice which has used the judge as its 'Nimitta' and he is blameless.

"A man's thinking should be entirely devoid of selfish desires. It should be spurred by wisdom and knowledge. He should renounce the benefits resulting from his actions. Such a man will ever be happy and whatever he does will be yajna. He who is free of all desires, who is able to keep his mind under control, who has withdrawn his mind from the objects of the senses, such a man is a Sanyasi though he is acting in the world of mankind. A man who is satisfied with anything which is meted out to him as his share, who is indifferent to happiness or sorrow, will never be caught in the snares of Karma. His intellect will be clear and he will act in the world for the good of mankind and nothing else will motivate his actions. He is performing yajna.

"Karma is born of the Brahman and so it should be understood that the result of an action which is offered to the Lord is itself the Brahman. When gifts are given away, the gifts again comprise the Brahman. To a man who knows this the Brahman has come within reach. Karma by itself has no significance. It acquires significance because of the purpose behind it, the rules which govern it, the limits imposed on it. The true merit lies in the performance of action conforming to divine laws. Karma becomes great when the performance is without an eye on the fruits of the action. The renunciation of the rewards of action define the greatness of Karma."

The Lord continued: "That ignorant man who is not earnest enough, who does not have enough faith, who is ever drowned in the sea of doubt, will have no place either in this world or in the next. The man beset with doubts will ever be unhappy as he chooses to be so."

The unrest in the mind of Arjuna was lifting gradually but the process was not complete. Krishna was keen to convince Arjuna that a life of action was ideally suited for him. It was necessary to steady the mind of Arjuna so that he could realize that he was a Kshatriya and that it was his duty to fight. This would lead to his taking up the Gandiva in his hand and making up his mind to do his duty. In the early moments of despair Arjuna had said that he would go back to the forests and become a Sanyasi. Krishna knew that it was not natural for him to act thus. Arjuna's mind was now withdrawn from thoughts of Sanyasa no doubt. But the words of Krishna reiterating the glories of Karma yoga had not made their full impact on him yet. The words of Krishna were still just a jumble of words to him and he could not sort them out.

He asked: "Krishna, at times you praise the glories of Sanyasa and at other times you talk about the superiority of action. Have pity on the confused state of my mind and tell me which of these two is better."

Krishna said: "Arjuna, both are good and both will bring you peace. But, if one were to choose between the two, I say that Karma yoga is better than Karmasanyasa. One does not become a Sanyasi merely by donning saffron robes and retreating into the cave of Himavan. He is the one who hates nothing nor is attached to anything. He is beyond the influence of the opposites, meaning, good and bad have no effect on him. Such a man will find release from bondage very soon. Only the ignorant find any difference between Karma and Sanyasa. In reality, the wise have known that the pursuit of either of these paths will grant the reward of both of them. The really wise man will find the unity between the two opposites paths, Sankhya and Karma yoga, between Nivritti and Pravritti. But the path of Sanyasa is hard to tread. The Karma yogi reaches the Brahmi state very soon. If he is wise, if he is able to control his mind, if he is able to see his Atman reflected in all those around him, he will be untainted by the world and he is the ideal yogi. And so, I repeat, Karma yoga is superior to Sanyasa."

From the beginning to the end Krishna has tried in different words to explain this theory of Karma yoga and he has elaborated on the paths Pravritti and Nivritti. So long as Arjuna remained in doubt Krishna did not lose patience but continued to instruct him on the secret of Karma yoga. Hence the repetition of the words: "Act without being concerned about the fruits of your actions." He wanted Arjuna to grasp the spirit of Karma yoga.

"With a pure mind, with the senses completely under control, with no thought for the fruits of one's actions, with complete indifference to the emotions of love and hatred, with only thoughts of the welfare of mankind spurring him on, man should keep doing his duties in the world and he should offer everything to the Lord. Such a man is a Karma yogi in the real sense of the word and this karma is really yajna which he is performing everyday."

The Welfare of the World

Sage Narada had told Vyasa: "My friend, in the epic Mahabharata stress has been laid on Karma yoga. But you have not paid enough attention to Bhakti. This is the reason why you have not been able to attain the peace you have been seeking. If you now compose a poem which propagates Bhakti in the heart of man, you would then have completed the task you have undertaken for the welfare of the world." Accordingly Vyasa is said to have composed the Bhagavata.

But the Gita is part of the Mahabharata and the Gita deals in great detail with the Bhakti marga. And so it is not quite right to say that the epic is lacking in Bhakti. The message of the Gita is the propagation of the Bhagavata dharma which is but a combination of Karma and Bhakti yogas. But one has to admit that Bhakti as dealt with in the Gita is different from that in the Bhagavata. The Bhakti in the Gita is not emotional. It is based more on intellectual arguments and discussions while Bhakti as it appears in the Bhagavata is purely emotional.

In every chapter where Krishna talks on Karma yoga he does talk of Bhakti, too. And the twelfth chapter of the Gita is named "Bhakti Yoga". It goes without saying that this chapter deals entirely with Bhakti as handled by the Gitacharya.

Arjuna asks Krishna for a description of a bhakta. And

Krishna answers him in great detail. "The bhakta worships the absolute truth, the Brahman which is eternal, which cannot be defined, which is not manifested, which cannot be grasped by the intellect, which is the permanent truth on which is based this entire creation. He treats everyone alike, he has no likes and dislikes. He has conquered the senses and he is bent only on the good of others. Such a bhakta will soon attain oneness with the Paramatma. But this type of worship is not easy. For a human being, for a worshipper who has a body, mind and intellect, it is difficult to think of the Brahman and concentrate on It." Krishna then speaks about the worship of the Saguna Brahman and adds that it is a path far easier than Jnana yoga.

Krishna tells Arjuna: "This path is not very different from the path of Karma which I have been talking about. My bhakta should dedicate everything to me. He should contemplate on me and worship only me. I will soon release him from the bondage of worldliness. And so, Arjuna, let your thoughts flow towards me in a continuous stream like the flow of the river towards the sea. If your mind is set on me you will soon become part of me. You will become lost in me and there is no doubt about it.

"I will describe my bhakta to you. He has no hatred towards anyone. He has nothing but love for all human beings. He is compassionate and in him the feelings of "I" and "MINE" have perished long ago. He is beyond the reach of emotions like happiness and sorrow. Full of forgiveness, ever contented, always active, firm in his resolve, he has his mind and thoughts lost in me. Such a man is my bhakta and he is very dear to me. The world cannot wield any influence on him nor can he agitate the world around him. Gladness, impatience, fear and excitement have no place in his heart. He has no desire and he is pure in body and mind. Dexterity in actions will be his and he will rise above the level of desires. He has no sadness in his mind. He does not consider that he is responsible for any act of his but dedicates it all to me. He is never given to excesses of happiness or hatred but he treats them alike. The good or bad results of his actions do not affect him as he has ever been indifferent to the results of his actions. Friend and foe seem alike and even so, honor and disgrace or insults. The ailments of the body do not affect him and he is devoid of all attachment. Censure or praise mean the same to him. Sparse of speech, he is ever contented and devoid of attachment to the things of this world. His mind is firm and he is devoted to me."

These characteristics of a bhakta are enumerated in detail by Krishna for the benefit of Arjuna. It is clear that the description of a bhakta and that of a Sthithaprajna is almost identical. The description of the evolved soul who is beyond the reach of the gunas is also the same. There is no difference between a bhakta and the Sthithaprajna. Krishna has raised Bhakti to such a level that one is amazed at the distance in time he has traveled from the sands on the banks of the Yamuna where he danced the Rasa with the gopis to the field of battle where he describes a bhakta and the qualities essential for him. The distance is that of a star from another star. The truth is, neither a Karma yogi nor a bhakta can achieve his purpose easily. It is only by a complete control of the senses, by cleansing the mind of the opposites and conforming to the rigid rules and conditions imposed on him that man can aspire to be a Karma yogi or a bhakta.

On the other hand, there is the man who is engaged in performing a yajna according to the rites of the Karma Kanda. Different materials are collected: ghee, oil, til, grains and several other things are offered to the fire which is blazing. Mantras are chanted by the priests who promise to him that the gates of the heavens will be opened to him. If the man believes this he is only deceiving himself. The materials have been burnt and turned to ashes and the yajna has been performed according to the Vedic rites. But this is not Karma yoga. The entire life of a man is a yajna. This is the roaring fire and the offerings to be made to this sacrificial fire are the good actions which should be done with a desire to benefit the world. A Karma yogi whose acts are according to the conditions imposed on him by the Lord is, in fact, performing nothing else but a yajna and his entire life is a yajna.

If a man is naive enough to believe that like Ajamila he will also find a place in heaven by just pronouncing the name of the Lord once on his deathbed, or by repeating the name of Rama thousands of times with a mala in hand, if he expects the attendants of Naryana to approach him and take him straight to the presence of the Lord, he is sadly mistaken. He is cheating himself.

The path of a bhakta is not all that easy. It is hard in the beginning, but gets easier as one proceeds. It is like the saying: "Like poison in the beginning which becomes nectar in the end." The paths trod by a bhakta and that trod by a Karma yogi are identical. They are not strewn with flowers and pleasures. The first requirment for a traveler in the path towards the Brahman is the renunciation of all pleasures and the desire for them too. This will be hard in the beginning, but once it is mastered the path becomes easier. Once man has attained this, other things look small and meaningless to him. Once the Brahmi state is reached, the greatest of misfortunes can befall him but it will cease to appear so to him. He will stand firm and undaunted under any circumstances.

The price he has to pay to tread these paths is not small by any means. The Yoga is expensive as man has to give up everything he has to proceed in this path.

The twelfth chapter is devoted to Bhakti yoga. But in the Gita this is not the sole chapter on Bhakti. In every chapter Karma and Bhakti have always been coupled together and mention is often made of them as one. "Abandoning all attachment, hatred, fear, set your mind on me. Take refuge in me. You will be purified by Jnana and such people will reach me," says Krishna. Again he says: "He who considers me as the recipient of all the yajnas and tapas, the Lord of all the worlds and his well-wisher, such a man will attain peace."

And, "One who dwells on me constantly and worships is a Yogi and he can rest assured that I will take care of his Yoga."

And, "Anything you do, whether it is an action, eating, or worship, whether it is a gift to someone or even tapas, dedicate them all to me."

In the tenth chapter the Lord has recounted all His Vibhutis to establish Bhakti firmly in the mind of His devotee. The eleventh chapter contains the vision of His Cosmic form, His Vishvaroopa. Further on, He again repeats the statement: "With single-mindedness if a man worships me he will traverse the three gunas and reach the Brahmi state."

The entire Gita is devoted to the dissertation on these two Yogas. Some slokas deal with the one and some with the other; they are always together in the Gita.

Slowly Arjuna sheds his unwillingness to fight but he keeps on asking questions as he has now become absorbed in the teachings of Krishna. He asks: "Krishna, explain to me once again the entire truth about Sanyasa and the lesson of renunciation."

Patiently Krishna resumes his discourse and says: "Work is performed with a desire for the results, with a selfish motive. The renunciation of this desire or this selfish motive constitutes Sanyasa: being indifferent to the results of one's actions is renunciation. Some teachers have stipulated that all action is sinful and so should be given up. Some others have said that yajnas, charity, tapas, should not be given up. But according to me, there is but one truth. To be without action is not possible for a human being and so the only path open to him is to renounce the results of his actions. As long as a man is unable to give up his ego, 'Ahambhava', his mind will not escape involvement in the world. The first essential step is to renounce this Ahambhava. The action of man will then become disinterested and even if he kills anyone the sin does not cling to him. The man who performs his daily duties will attain salvation by this path alone.

"Even if one's duty makes unpleasant tasks unavoidable, still one should not shirk from duty. If there is no desire for the results of the action, if it is performed in the manner spoken by me, then the sin in committing the act which seems sinful will not cling to him. One whose Atman can become part of the Paramatma will have no desires, no worries in his mind. In his eyes all beings will appear to be the same and such a man is my bhakta. While doing his duties he has sought refuge in me and so eternal peace will be his."

The conversation had gone on for a while now and Krishna wanted to end it with some concluding remarks. He said: "Arjuna, listen very carefully. If you follow my words, all your difficulties will vanish. But if you allow your ego to gain ascendancy over you and let it prompt you to ignore my words then you will be destroyed. If, because of your ego, you say: 'I will not fight,' meaning that you will not do your duty, your words will then sound false because it is your nature as a Kshatriya to fight and no man can fight nature. In spite of you, nature, Svabhava, will drag you towards action.

Man is a slave to his nature. He is bound by it and so I tell you, even if you are averse to it, you will have to act in the world according to your Svabhava. The Lord dwells in the heart of every one of us and it is He who makes you act in this world. Abandon your ego, Arjuna, make an offering of your actions to me and their results too, and pursue your duties. Set your mind on me. Worship me and make your salutations to me. And you will become one with me. I promise this to you, that it will be so. End this discussion and come to me for refuge. Do not worry as I will protect you till the very end. Arjuna, are you rid of your doubts now?"

Arjuna was enlightened by the words of Krishna. "Yes," he said. "My doubts have all been cleared. I will do what you ask me to do. I will do my duty as commanded by you."

When we review the Gita in its completeness there are four descriptions which come to the mind. We have the description of the Sthithaprajna in the second chapter; that of the bhakta in the twelfth chapter; the detailed description of the soul which is beyond the reach of the gunas which occurs in the fourteenth chapter; and, finally, in the sixteenth chapter is described the man endowed with divinity. All these refer to the same person because each quality tends to emphasize the other. Each is a repetition of the other.

In the Gita, Krishna has taught the philosophy of Karma not only to Arjuna but to entire mankind. Yet this nectar which he holds out cannot be forced down anyone's throat. The man who wants to be free from bondage has to undo the knots by himself and the task is by no means easy. If he ignores the insistence that he should do it himself, then the study of the Gita or any other sacred book will prove to be of no use whatever to him.

The paths set down for the Karma yogi and the bhakta should not dishearten the aspirant because of the difficulty in practicing them. Self-realization is not impossible. The path is hard for the idle man but not for the man who makes a genuine attempt. In short, the essence of the teachings of the Gita can be condensed into a few sentences which describe the Karma yoga.

Never should a man try to evade the performing of his duties. He should work with earnestness. The motive should be the welfare of mankind. The results of the actions should be ignored. The senses should be under control and they should not be allowed to pursue the world of objects which gratify them. The mind and the intellect should again be under perfect control. The aspirant should have but one thought in his mind: that the act and its results should be an offering to the Lord. The opposites should be avoided. They should be treated equally—pleasure and pain, censure or approbation, happiness and sorrow—and they should not have any effect on him.

Krishna finally says: "I have spoken and it is now up to you to make up your mind and do what you wish."

"I am cured . . ." says Arjuna. "I will obey your commands and I will do what I must do."

In its essence the Gita in all its eighteen chapters teaches us the lesson that plurality does not exist. The waters of the ocean, its waves, every drop of water in it are all but one. Even so, one power and only one pervades the entire universe and there is no cause here for thoughts of plurality. The meaning of the Mahavakyas, "I am the Brahman . . ." and "You are that . . ." means this.

Vyasa by his grace had granted Sanjaya the power to know what was going on when the war began. Even from a distance he could see everything and he could enter into the minds of all and know their thoughts. He was recounting everything to the blind king Dhritarashtra.

Sanjaya listened to the Gita as expounded by Krishna and the effect on him was profound. He said: "My lord, the hearing of this divine conversation between Krishna and Arjuna has ennobled and elevated me. I remember the Vishvaroopa of the Lord; the wonderment of it has not left me yet. I am thrilled by it and I am living those sublime moments over and over, again and again. I have gathered the truth from the words of Krishna. Where the great Yogeshvara, Krishna, is present, and where the greatest of archers, Arjuna, is, there will be found beauty, goodness, and the bliss of the manifestation of the Lord. There will be Dharma present and purity as well as peace. I am certain of it."

Krishna in the Two Poems

We have already been told that Vyasa composed the Bhagavata after the Mahabharata at the suggestion of Narada. Krishna was responsible for the reestablishment of the Bhagavata dharma. Both the poems lay emphasis on Karma yoga and Bhakti yoga. Though both poems deal with the same sentiment, Bhakti as handled in the Bhagavata is different from that in the Mahabharata. In the treatment of Bhakti in the Mahabharata, Vedanta as well as the play of the intellect have been given greater importance. This difference arises from the fact that Krishna in the one poem is different from Krishna in the other. If one were to study the characterization of Krishna in the Mahabharata this difference is very clear. Krishna of the Bhagavata has to be WORSHIPPED while Krishna of the Mahabharata is to be considered an EXAMPLE to be emulated.

Vyasa composed the Bhagavata which, to a large extent, deals with the Bhakti marga. The main character in this poem is Krishna. Vyasa has said in so many words that Krishna is Lord Narayana himself and he has related stories about Krishna in a manner which instills bhakti in the minds of the readers. The greatness of Krishna is evident from the narration of these many incidents in his life.

Perhaps it may not be known to some that this avatara of the Lord as Krishna is the twenty-fourth avatara. Later, there is no thought that he is an avatara at all but Narayana himself. If enough attention is not paid to this fact, one is apt only to worship him and to forget that Krishna was a great personage. Only thoughts of worship occur in the minds of the readers of Bhagavata and there is no desire in them to make him an example to be followed.

The entire framework of the Mahabharata is different. It is unique. The purpose of the poem is different too. Great characters have been portrayed in it and their many qualities have been dealt with in great detail. We come to the conclusion that however highly or lowly placed a man may be, his life is meant for the good of mankind, and his life should be a lesson to the men who come after. With this purpose in mind, Vyasa has blended teaching of morality and conduct in a manner so wonderful that the impact made on the minds of readers has lasted even till today.

While sketching the characters in the Mahabharata, the poet has not tried to soften the weaknesses in those who are worthy of respect nor does he overlook the goodness in those who are not so venerable. This achievement of Vyasa is memorable. He is a genius in this art of characterization and the examples of greatness whom he has set before us should be studied again and again. This book is ageless and men of all times will benefit by the study of it; it is a book for all times.

Among the characters in the Mahabharata, Krishna is the most attractive and the most interesting. Studying him and stories about him will make our journey through life easy. He is a complex character. If, for a moment, we ignore the fact that he is an avatara, the complexity and beauty of it is even more fascinating. Scholars have paid particular attention to the character of Krishna and much has been written about him. For the bhaktas the proper subject is Krishna of the Bhagavata as it is only worship of the divine which prompts them to think of him. If, however, one wants to know of a life which can ennoble others, if the desire is to emulate such a life, then the character of Krishna as portrayed in the Mahabharata will prove to be the ideal life to be studied. One will realize why the rishis have called Krishna by the names Dheera, Buddha, Kavi, Prajna, Pandita and Yogeshvara.

Vyasa's interpretation of Krishna is not an avatara but a great and wise character.

Krishna had great affection for the Padavas. His first meeting with them is after the Swayamvara of Draupadi in Panchala. The Swayamvara hall was crowded with the kings of Bharatavarsha, each vying with the other for the hand of the princess who was divine by birth. Krishna was there with the Yadava host. Krishna did not make any attempt to try his hand at the Matsya yantra which had been set up as a challenge for the archers of the day. This seemed strange to the others. But Krishna refrained because he had a strong feeling that the Pandavas would be present there. Though he had not met them, there was in his mind a feeling of affection for these cousins of his. He thought kindly of them. He knew about the injustice which had been done to them by the Kauravas.

Kunti, the mother of the Pandavas, was his aunt, the sister of Vasudeva. So there was a close blood relationship between the Pandavas and Krishna and yet, strangely enough, their first meeting was only during the Swayamvara of Draupadi. They had not met all these years. After their first meeting their kinship became more firm and there was forged between them a friendship which has no parallel in history or in any other story except, perhaps, the friendship between Duryodhana and Karna. The Pandavas became extremely dear to Krishna, especially Arjuna, who owed almost his very life to Krishna. The affection and the partiality of Krishna for the Pandavas was only too well known. At times Krishna even took recourse to "deceit" to assist the Pandavas. There are several incidents in the Mahabharata to illustrate this "injustice of Love" which Krishna felt towards the Pandavas.

After the wedding of Draupadi with all the five brothers, Bheeshma, the grand old man of the Kaurava court, along with other wise men, accosted Dhritarashtra. Bheeshma advised the old blind king against nursing hatred towards the sons of Pandu, who were his nephews. The king was made to realize that the Pandevas were not to be ignored, related as they were to the powerful Drupada, the king of the Panchalas. Dhritarashtra was afraid for his sons and he agreed to divide the kingdom between his son and Yudhishthira. Khandavaprastha was the share which fell to Yudhishthira and there he established his kingdom.

The piece of land was a desert, a barren and neglected expanse which bore a curse on it. Krishna was angry with the injustice in the division of the land. He called Indra and asked him to change the face of the country. Indra sent rain and made the land fruitful and green. The land, which had no water nor any vegetation to speak of, was now rich, fruitful and beautiful because of the grace of Indra. Yudhishthira changed the name of Khandavaprastha to Indraprastha to honor Indra whose bounty was responsible for this new life to the land. He ruled the kingdom wisely and well and he was loved by his subjects.

Krishna, the Superman

An incident occurred as a result of which Arjuna had to undertake a Tirthayatra, a pilgrimage to the holy spots in the land. During the yatra Arjuna went to the southernmost end of the country and then commenced his journey homewards. His mind went to Swaraka, the city of Krishna. It was not just to see Krishna that he wanted to go there. He had another desire which prompted him to think of Dwaraka.

Arjuna had heard about the beauty and charm of the maiden Subhadra, Krishna's sister. He had been attracted by her even before he had seen her and the wish to see her was what spurred his thoughts toward Dwaraka.

Arjuna was eager to see Subhadra, but he did not want to be seen by anyone and be recognized as Arjuna. He decided to disguise himself. He smeared sacred ashes all over his body and took up a trident in his hand. Dressed in ochre robes, this spurious Sanyasi entered the city of Dwaraka. Just on the outskirts of the city he sat under the shade of a tree. He adopted the Padmasana, the posture of the Yatis and, with his eyes closed, Arjuna sat there as though he were in deep meditation.

People soon became aware of the presence of a Sanyasi in the city and his fame spread all over Dwaraka. The citizens arrived in flocks to have a darshan of this young Sanyasi who sat with his eyes always closed, who was ever lost in meditation, who had no thoughts of this world.

Balarama, the elder son of Vasudeva, also came to have a darshan of the Yati. He was not able to see through the disguise of Arjuna. And Krishna had come too, with Balarama, but he would not be taken in by the guise of Arjuna. When they were alone Krishna asked him: "Arjuna, what has happened? What is the game you are trying to play?"

Arjuna said: "Why do you ask? Of course you know full well that I am in love with your sister Subhadra and I want to marry her. I depend on you to help me and so I have come here."

Krishna said: "I will help you. But then, you should first make sure that Subhadra also is interested in you and that she desires this alliance. If it is so, you are at liberty to carry her away. This is the custom among Kshatriyas and you can follow it."

In the meantime, the "Yati" had made a great impression on Balarama. He suggested that the Yati should be asked to stay in the apartments of Subhadra and that she should attend to his wants in order to get his blessings. Krishna was secretly pleased with the suggestion, but pretended not to agree with his brother. He said: "We know nothing about this Yati. We do not know what kind of man he is. How can you be certain that he is a good man? I do not approve of his residing in the apartments of young women, of Subhadra in particular. This man seems to be young and handsome. Our Subhadra is young and is at an impressionable age. It is not proper that they should be thrown together."

Balarama would not hear a word against the Yati. He chided Krishna and said: "It is sinful even to think such thoughts about a great man like him."

Finally, the Yati was established in the apartments of Subhadra. The princess did not of course know who he was. She had heard of Arjuna, the Pandava, from her brother, from her cousins, Gada, Samba and others, who had known him. Several stories had been told her about his prowess, his skill in archery, his looks and his charm. She had been attracted by these stories and she had made up her mind that she would marry only Arjuna.

While serving the Yati she once asked him: "My lord, you

have traveled in many countries. Have you, at any time during your wanderings, come across the Pandava prince by name Arjuna? How does he look? I have heard so much about him and I would like to hear about him from you."

Arjuna did not want to hide the fact from her any longer as he felt that it would be wrong. He said: "Princess, Arjuna is seated right here, in front of you, and he has adopted the guise of a Yati for the sake of his love for you."

Arjuna was infatuated with Subhadra and she had the same feelings for him. When she realized that the Yati was Arjuna she felt that she should not come to him any more and she stopped her visits. Arjuna was suffering agonies because of this and did not know what to do. Subhadra was so near and yet so far from him. He was suffering because of the separation from her, and Rukmini took it upon herself to attend on him, but he was not pleased with this.

Subhadra was also pining away. Rukmini, who knew the whole story, went to Krishna and told him about the suffering of the young princess because of her love for Arjuna. Arjuna was, of course, inconsolable! Krishna felt that something drastic should be done if his sister was to be happy. He therefore went to his brother with a suggestion. He said: "There is an island nearby where there is a temple of Siva. If we perform pooja to him for two weeks, our sister's illness will be cured." Balarama was willing to accept the suggestion and everyone was happy to go on this pilgrimage. All the heroes of the Yadava clan left Dwaraka and went to the island to worship Siva. Arjuna and Subhadra were left all alone in Dwaraka.

Before he left, Krishna went to his sister and said: "My dear child, I know how it is with you. Twelve days from today is an auspicious day. Arjuna and you should get married on that particular day. I am going now and the rest I have left in the hands of you both. I have spoken to Arjuna about everything. You have my blessings." He comforted the weeping girl who had fallen at his feet and went with the other Yadavas to worship Siva.

On the appointed day Arjuna said: "Subhadra, it is twelve days since they all left for the island to worship Siva. Krishna must have told you that we have to be married today and his blessings are with us. We are Kshatriyas and the Gandharva type of marriage is allowed. We will be married accordingly. Get the chariot ready and leave with me for Indraprastha."

Subhadra made all the preparations. Before he left Krishna had taken care to leave his chariot behind and this was fully equipped with all the weapons needed by a warrior. Subhadra was very good at driving a chariot. And so, with Subhadra holding the reins in her hand, Arjuna sat in the chariot of Krishna. She placed the whip lightly on the flanks of the horses and they ran swiftly carrying them away from Dwaraka. The gatekeepers saw that someone was taking Subhadra with him. He was like Arjuna, and they created an uproar and tried to stop the chariot, but it was not possible.

News reached the Yadavas that Subhadra had been carried away and that the Yati was missing. They came back to Dwaraka in a hurry. Full of fury, Balarama and the others made all preparations to capture Arjuna. Balarama said: "I will kill all the Pandavas. I will raze Indraprastha to the ground." Krishna stood silent listening to the words of everyone. Balarama asked him: "Why are you silent, Krishna? I have a feeling that you have had a hand in this conspiracy."

Krishna tried to look as innocent as possible and said: "My beloved brother, I told you long ago that this was an unwise thing to do, leaving them together. I stressed on the youth of both and the susceptibility of a young maiden to the handsomeness and the youth of the Yati. But you would not pay heed to my words. What is the use of becoming angry now? It is now evident that they are in love with each other. As for Arjuna, he is a worthy husband for our sister. He is a hero, he is our kinsman and he is a Kshatriya. Is it possible to get a better groom for our Subhadra even if we tried? Nothing untoward has happened. Let us forget our anger and bless the young lovers." Balarama saw the wisdom in the words of Krishna and was pacified.

Arjuna reached Indraprastha. With the permission and the blessings of Draupadi and his brothers he married Subhadra. By then Balarama, Krishna and the other Yadavas arrived in Indraprastha laden with gifts. Subhadra was happy that there was no unpleasantness because of her conduct and she knew that she had to thank Krishna for it.

In this episode it is obvious that all three of them, Krishna, Arjuna and Subhadra were guilty of deceit. But it is not possible to blame them and say that they did wrong. Krishna summed it up with the words: "Arjuna is a hero, our kinsman, a Kshatriya, a warrior and a worthy youngster. And they love each other. What is wrong with their elopement?"

The affair was innocent, no doubt, but the dealings had to be underhand and subterfuge was needed for managing it. Krishna was a past master at it. But he did nothing which was against the code of honor or righteousness.

This is but one example of the many facets of Krishna's character. There are several incidents in the full and varied life of Krishna where he had to resort to deceit. From the point of view of honor, they were all correct and were not wrong. If one were to study the life of this great man again and again, one becomes more and more convinced that he is an avatara and not just a great man.

What is an avatara? An avatara purusha is meant to lead men in the right path; to instill in them a feeling of rightness. This is why a man possessed of a great intellect, who has visions of the future, is born to suppress evil and such a leader grants happiness to the oppressed. Character and wisdom cannot be found in a man of small intelligence. And so, in an avatara purusha, several qualities have to be found —cleverness in dealing with situations which are difficult and endowed with a sense of justice and righteousness. Such a man was Krishna.

The incident of Subhadra and Arjuna has been related in a condensed form by me. But this is not the sole instance from the life of Krishna where he reveals his genius in manipulating affairs cleverly. In the Mahabharata there are several occasions where he has, for the welfare of mankind, used all his quickness of mind and thought and subterfuge. And never once do we feel that he did wrong.

Justice and Mercy

In those days when the Pandavas reigned, it was customary for a king to perform a yaga called Rajasuya to announce to the world that he was supreme. He had to conquer all the other kings to establish his sovereignty. After the coronation of Yudhishthira in Indraprastha, several people who were near to him suggested that he should perform the Rajasuya. Yudhishthira was peace-loving by nature and he did not relish the suggestion. Bhima and Arjuna, however, were very much in favor of it. Yudhishthira said: "If I have to perform the yaga I will have to fight with several kings and after defeating them declare that I am the emperor. There will be much killing which is unnecessary. It is not a pleasing thought.

"Apart from my feelings in the matter, fighting with other kings means fighting with Jarasandha. He cannot be ignored. It is only too well-known that he is extremely powerful. How can he be defeated? The yajna cannot be performed unless he is vanquished. The best thing will be to forget about the Rajasuya altogether."

Bhima said: "Arjuna and I, with the help of Krishna, can certainly accomplish this task which seems to be difficult to you, dear brother. Are we not powerful enough to do so?"

Krishna intervened and said: "Bhima, evidently you are not quite aware of the strength of Jarasandha. He is a righteous man and he is very generous by nature. He is a great bhakta of Siva. It will be a hard task fighting him, leave alone killing him. There is only one reason strong enough to goad us into this fight. Jarasandha has captured hundreds of kings and they are all his captives. He is planning to conduct a sacrifice of these kings to please Siva. And so, even when I know that it will be hard to kill Jarasandha, we should take him on at least to save the unfortunate kings."

Yudhishthira was still hesitant about it and would not give his consent easily to the venture. Bhima and Arjuna stressed the fact that the unfortunate kings were harassed by the tyrant Jarasandha and their misery should come to an end. The sacrifice which he had planned had to be stopped at any cost. Krishna also supported the younger brothers of Yudhishthira and added: "It will be impossible to approach Jarasandha with an army and try to defeat him in open fighting. Indra himself would find it difficult. But I have different plans to achieve our ends. If it is possible to arrange a duel between Bhima and Jarasandha, our Bhima may be able to kill him. A touch of deceit is, of course, essential and I can manage that."

Finally Yudhishthira agreed to send them to Magadha.

When they reached the outskirts of Girivraja, the capital of Magadha, Krishna and the Pandava brothers abandoned their silks and donned the guise of snatakas. And they placed garlands of flowers on their necks and applied sandal paste to their arms and chests. Dressed thus they went to the city of Girivraja. When they neared the palace they went to the back and, jumping over the wall, they entered it. There was a rule in ancient times that the enemy's city should not be entered by the main gate nor should one use the front door of his house. They sent word to the king that they had come to meet him. Jarasandha was engaged in the worship of Siva. When he was told that three snatakas had come to see him he sent word that he could grant them an audience at midnight.

As per his promise Jarasandha went to meet them at midnight. He was very courteous to them. But there was a look of doubt on his face as he stood before them. He said: "You say that you are snatakas and you are dressed that way too. But the garlands of flowers and the perfume you are wearing makes me doubt that you are snatakas; you appear to be Kshatriyas. This youngster has scars on his shoulders which can be seen only on an archer. You have avoided entering my palace from the front entrance and your behavior is unusual. I sent food to you but that has been left untouched, I am told. Tell me, who are you? Why have you come here? My welcome to you is wholehearted as you have chosen to be my guests. But you do not seem to be holding out the hand of friendship to me."

Krishna spoke: "Jarasandha, you speak the truth. We happen to be your enemies and we have come here seeking a fight with you. This is the reason why we could not partake of the food which you had sent us. Food should not be eaten in the house of the enemy."

Jarasandha had a puzzled look on his face. He said: "I do not know you. How can you be my enemies? I do not remember having seen you before, ever. If you persist in calling yourselves my enemies, tell me who you are and what is the bone of contention between you and me."

Again it was Krishna who spoke. He said: "Our enmity rises out of the fact that you have, without reason, placed several kings in captivity. They have not offended you in any way and your action is unjust. We know that you are planning to sacrifice these kings. This is sinful and we cannot tolerate it. It is the duty of a righteous king to prevent injustice and to help those who are helpless. We do not want to hide our identities from you. This young man whom you recognized as an archer, is Arjuna, the Pandava, and this is Bhima, his brother. Both of them, as you must have guessed, are the brothers of the king Yudhishthira. As for me, I am an old acquaintance of yours, Krishna. You are at liberty to choose one of us and give us fight."

Jarasandha laughed loudly when he heard the words of Krishna. He turned to Krishna with a look of utter contempt and said: "Eighteen times have I defeated you in battle and you have run away from me every time to save your skin. Now you are in Dwaraka because you want to escape from me. How can I fight with you? It is beneath my dignity to fight with a coward like you. What surprises me is the courage with which you have appeared before me to ask me to give you fight! Never once have you been able to stand in front of me. I am not Kamsa whom you killed by deceit. I do not wish to fight with you. If I do so, it will win for me infamy in the days to come. As for Arjuna, he seems to be but a child. It is not fair to fight with him. I choose Bhima who seems to be the fittest."

As he prepared himself to fight, Jarasandha saw evil omens. Some premonition made him pause for a moment. He called his young son Sahadeva to his side and in haste he made him the yuvaraja. The child was placed on the throne and after that Jarasandha came out to fight with Bhima.

The fight was on. Both were warriors of no mean order and they were evenly matched. Krishna knew that Bhima would tire soon and so he went on encouraging him in loud terms. He said: "Bhima, remember you are the son of Vayu. You have immense strength in you and do not slacken in your efforts to vanquish your enemy." Bhima heard the words of Krishna and new strength seemed to flow in his arms when he thought of Vayu.

Bhima lifted Jarasandha above his head and with great effort he caught the two legs of his victim and tore him apart. He threw the halves on the ground and looked at Krishna triumphantly. He saw a horrified look on the face of Arjuna and he looked where he was gazing. The two halves of Jarasandha had touched each other and at once they joined together and Jarasandha was whole again, ready to fight. There was a smile of triumph on his face. This was a special boon granted to Jarasandha that the two halves of his body, if they were close enough, would join together and he would become whole once again. And so he baffled the efforts of Bhima.

Again and again Bhima tore him apart and the same frustrating experience was there: he would be rejoined again and ready to fight.

Bhima was now getting tired. Krishna managed to catch the attention of Bhima. They had been fighting in the palace gardens. Krishna casually pulled a leaf from the plantain tree nearby, and tearing it into two he threw the pieces far from each other. Bhima understood what he meant. He now tore Jarasandha and threw the halves into two opposite corners.

As they were far apart, the two pieces could not rejoin and Jarasandha was dead. There was great uproar when this happened. His men did not know what they should do. They had never imagined that their king would be killed and panic was spreading everywhere.

Krishna spoke to them in a soft and gentle voice and calmed them. He said: "We have no cause to fight with any of you. We were here to avert an injustice and we have done so. You need have no fear that we will destroy all of you."

They ascended the chariot of Jarasandha and went to the hill fort Girivraja. The kings had been imprisoned there. Krishna went to the cells and released them. They were speechless with relief and surprise. They could not believe that their captivity had ended and that they were free now. They said: "Lord Krishna, how can we show our gratitude to you for saving our lives?"

Krishna said: "I ask for nothing. In a few days king Yudhishthira will be performing theRajasuya. You should attend it as the allies of the king. You should be the guests of the king. That is the only way you can show your gratitude to me and to the brothers of king Yudhishthira."

Krishna then went to Sahadeva, the young son of the dead king, and said: "Do not be afraid, child. You are now the king of Magadha. Be like your father in strength and in prowess. Remember to walk in the path of Dharma always."

Sahadeva was very humble and he said: "I am grateful to you for your words of affection. I will be present at the Rajasuya of the king and I will remember your injunctions about righteousness."

The killing of Jarasandha was a great event. There are several things to be noted here. The foremost is the subterfuge of Krishna, the deceit adopted by the three of them. And again, alongside can be seen the sense of justice, the desire to punish the Adharmi and to protect the oppressed. The incident reveals to us the genius of Krishna, his skill in maneuvering things in order to achieve what he wants, and his sense of justice too.

Krishna in Kamyakavana

Jarasandha was the main hurdle who had to be overcome and that was accomplished. There was now nothing to prevent Yudhishthira from making preparations for the Rajasuya. Arjuna and his brothers went out into the different quarters and came back with the news that all the kings had willingly agreed to accept Yudhishthira as the emperor. There were reasons for this acceptance. Yudhishthira was a good king and he was righteous. The entire Bharatavarsha knew about the many misfortunes of the Pandavas before their establishing a kingdom in Indraprastha. The kings were all very happy at the good fortune of Yudhishthira and they were only too happy to attend the Rajasuya and bless him.

The yaga was performed with great pomp and it was coming to an end. When the guests were to be honored there was the question of choosing the best among them so that he could be honored first. This was a custom to be observed.

Several names came to the minds of the kings there, but Beeshma put an end to all discussions by saying that Krishna was the best among them all and that he should be honored. He said: "In this large assembly, where many noble kings are present, it seems to me, Krishna shines as the noblest of all. He shines like the sun and the others are but the rays of the sun. Without him this hall will lose its lustre, its glory, and I claim again that Krishna has to be honored as the chief guest."

The Pandavas were thrilled that their grandfather had given expression to what was in their minds and they set about the pleasant task of honoring Krishna.

Some kings, however, were irked by this. Chief among them was Shishupala of Chedi. He stood up and spoke harshly and disparagingly of Krishna and tried to tell the assembly how unfit he was for the honor paid to him. His words were so sharp that the Pandavas could not brook the insult to their beloved Krishna. But Bheeshma asked them to calm down and told them that it had been ordained that Shishupala would meet his death at the hands of Krishna. He said: "The end of this sinful cousin of Krishna's is fast approaching." Bheeshma was not spared by Shishupala and the old man was insulted again and again by the arrogant king.

Krishna spoke to the assembled kings. He said: "Shishupala is the son of my aunt. I had promised my aunt that I would not pay any attention to the words of anger flung at me by her son as she is dear to me. But, I had also told her that I would tolerate only one hundred of his transgressions. She was pleased with me. For her sake I have been patient with this king. But I am afraid he has crossed the limit. The number hundred has been passed long ago and I have no other option." Then Krishna took up his chakra and cut off the head of Shishupala.

The incident left a mark in the minds of all of them. It seemed to be an evil omen. The sanctity of the yaga was marred by this incident. Yudhishthira was sorely distressed by it. He asked Vyasa, who was present there for the occasion: "Maharshi, it is evident that this incident promises nothing but unpleasantness in the days to come. Can you look into the future and tell me what is in store for us? I am afraid of the future."

Vyasa said: "Yudhishthira, you are right. The omens are not favorable. In the days to come, the sinfulness of Duryodhana, the valor of Bhima and Arjuna, the anger in the eyes of Draupadi who is the daughter of fire—all these will combine and bring about the destruction of the entire world. There is no use in your being distressed about it as what is ordained will come to pass. Nothing can stop the inexorable course of events in the days to come. The world will be destroyed and there is no doubt about it."

Everyone is only too familiar with what happened after this Rajasuya: Duryodhana's invitation to Yudhishthira to play a game of dice; the defeat of Yudhishthira in the game; the insult to Draupadi and the banishment of the Pandavas to the forest.

After he had taken leave of the Pandavas at the Rajasuya, Krishna's next meeting with them was in the Kamyakavana. He heard about the misfortunes of his cousins and he was very angry with Duryodhana and his associates. Many heroes of the Vrishni House were with him. Krishna was burning with anger when he met the Pandavas. He said: "Yudhishthira, I was not in Swaraka when all these things happened. I had to fight with Salva and when I was busy with the fighting, this deadly game of dice had been arranged in Hastina. If I had known about it I would have hurried to your side and I would have stopped you from playing the game which has robbed you of everything. I have brought my army with me. Now, at this very moment, let us attack Hastina and we can destroy the entire Kaurava host. Come, you know that the kings in the entire Bharatavarsha are with you and their sympathies are also with you. Let us put an end to this farce, this Vanavasa of yours, and capture the world. It rightly belongs to you."

Yudhishthira spoke in a soft, gentle, but firm voice. He tried to pacify Krishna and said: "Krishna, I am afraid it will not be possible for me to go back on my word. I have sinned and I have to suffer the consequences of that sin. I cannot break my promise and incur a further sin. I will go ahead with the punishment meted out to me."

Krishna could not be pacified. He said: "Yudhishthira! You and I are part of each other. Nothing cam come between us. You are mine and I am all yours. Your enemeis are my enemies and your firends are mine. I swear that I will not rest until I destroy all your enemies. I will drench this earth with the blood of these sinners. This is my oath, solemnly taken and I will achieve it."

Draupadi was standing there with tears in her eyes. She

said: "Krishna, I am the daughter of Drupada, a great hero, and I am the wife of five great heroes, the Pandavas. Their valor is said to be unequaled in all the three worlds but think of the manner in which I was treated in the court of the Kauravas."

Krishna lifted her face up. He wiped her tears and said: "Draupadi, be patient for just a while longer. I assure you that the women in the palaces of Hastina, the wives of those sinners, will all be shedding tears even as you are now. I swear to you that I will keep my oath. The sky may fall, or the earth broken into a thousand pieces, the great Himavan may, perhaps, melt and fall from its height, the earth may burst into a million splinters but the oath of Krishna will not be false. No one can stop me from my purpose. My dear sister, Draupadi, do not weep. I will, from now, think of nothing but the end of the Kauravas and all my efforts will be towards that end. I will have to wait for a while as your husband has decided to adhere to his promise to the Kauravas."

Krishna's anger had subsided after this outburst. He stayed on with the Pandavas for some more time and after assuring them that he would always come to them when they wanted him, he went back to Swaraka.

Yudhishthira Wanted Peace

The Pandavas spent twelve years in the forest and in accordance with the conditions of the exile they spent the thirteenth year incognito; and they spent it in the Matsya kingdom of which Virata was the capital city. The five brothers and Draupadi disguised themselves and lived in the court of the king.

There Bhima had to kill Keechaka. Duryodhana heard about it. But he could not guess that Bhima had accomplished this task as Bhima was in hiding. Duryodhana had, in the meantime, sent his men to all the four quarters of the earth to find our where the Pandavas were hiding. He was bent on the success of this mission as the discovery would drive the Pandavas to the forest for another twelve years. But much to his chagrin, the messengers from different spots came back without finding out anything about the Pandavas and their whereabouts.

Some were of the opinion that the killing of Keechaka could have been possible only for Bhima and suggested that Duryodhana should try and find out if the Pandavas were in Matsya. It was decided that Virata should be attacked and his cows stolen. If the Pandavas were there, this would make them come out of hiding as they would be obliged to help their host when he was in trouble.

The plan was carried out, the cows were stolen and there was fighting between the two armies. Arjuna, who was teaching dancing to the young princess, had to enter the field of battle to help the young prince Uttara and he managed to put the enemy to flight. This was, incidentally, the end of the year of the Ajnatavasa. The Pandavas could now come out into the open as they had fulfilled the conditions of their banishment.

A wedding had been arranged between Abhimanyu, the son of Arjuna, and the princess Uttara, the daughter of Virata. The Pandavas had invited all their friends and well-wishers to attend this wedding and naturally Balarama and Krishna were among those who were present.

After the celebrations were completed the next question on everyone's lips was: "What is to be done now?" The mind of each one of them was busy with thoughts on how the Pandavas were to get their kingdom back from the avaricious king Duryodhana. It was essential that justice should be meted out to the Pandavas and so a meeting of all the many kings who had come to attend the wedding was called. Everyone was asked to express his opinion. Finally Krishna stood up to address the assembly. Everyone was eager to listen to his words and silence prevailed in the hall when he rose to speak.

He said: "You are all familiar with the injustice done to the Pandavas by Duryodhana, and it is also known to all of you how the five princes with their queen spent these twelve years in the forest and this last year in the court of Virata. The game of dice which was played by Sakuni and the insult to Draupadi will not be forgotten by anyone in a hurry. Yudhishthira is a peaceloving man and never once has he expressed a desire to fight and regain his kingdom by force. All he wants is peace. The Pandavas are capable of defeating their enemies easily but they do not choose to fight. Yudhishthira, who had agreed to spend the thirteen years in exile as had been stipulated by his uncle and his cousin, is firmly set on the path of righteousness.

"The time has come now when this situation has to be reviewed. The time of reckoning has arrived and a decision is essential. You should all consider the future and advise the Pandavas. The decision should be such that the welfare of mankind is not forgotten. It should be fair and it should not be biased. Yudhishthira, as you all know, would rather renounce his rights to the kingdom than resort to injustice.

"The Kauravas have annexed the kingdom of Yudhishthira, which is his by right as a son of Pandu. By deceit he has been robbed of his kingdom. The kingdom was not lost in a fair battle where the winner gets the spoils. It was won in a game of dice, a game of deceit. It is not right.

"I do not have to recount to you about the many times when Dhritarashtra and Duryodhana have tried to ill-treat these young princes. Their heartless behavior is known to all of you: how the Pandavas were sent to Varanavata and their house was burnt withthe desire to destroy them.

"It is time this injustice is ended and righteousness established. Yudhisthira wants justice and he does not want war. We do not know what is favorable to Duryodhana. I suggest that a high-born Brahmin be sent to the court of Dhritarashtra and he should lay the facts before the elders in the court of the Kauravas. He should present the case and tell them that Yudhishthira is only asking that he should be treated with fairness. He is not fighting with his cousins."

Balarama agreed with the words of Krishna. But he was partial to Duryodhana and this was evident in the words he spoke. He said: "The message that the Pandavas want their share of the kingdom is right, but the messenger should be careful with the Kaurava host. He should be very humble and he should try and placate the elders by saluting them before addressing them. He should be careful not to use harsh language. Because the fact remains that Yudhishthira *did* lose his kingdom and that in a game of dice which he agreed to play. And so, while mentioning this incident, the messenger should be careful not to stress the deceit or injustice of the game. Yudhishthira should, very humbly, request that his share of the kingdom be given to him."

The kings assembled in the hall did not like the tone of Balarama's words. They could see that Duryodhana was responsible for creating this impression in his mind that there was no deceit in the game played long ago.

Yudhishthira could see, too, that Balarama was not quite pleased with the accusations aimed at Duryodhana and he was unhappy. Yet he spoke not a word. But Satyaki could not bear to hear those words and sit quiet. He jumped up and said: "I do not blame Balarama nor am I angry with him for these words spoken by him. I am only angry with those who have been listening to him and who still have not said a word in protest. If a messenger has to be sent to the court of the Kauravas let us not waste time sending inefficient men. Send me. I will go there, grasp Duryodhana by his forelocks, drag him here and toss him at the feet of Yudhishthira."

Everyone was pleased with the words of Satyaki because he spoke out what they felt. Drupada was glad that someone could get angry and heated about the situation and said: "Duryodhana is a sinner. As for the old men, Bheeshma and Drona, they have taken leave of their senses evidently or else they would not sit still as they are doing now. Evidently they are siding with Duryodhana. As for me, I do not object to a messenger being sent to plead our cause. Let the Brahmin go by all means. Let us see what happens."

Finally Krishna said: "Satyaki and Drupada have spoken the truth. But then, let us make every attempt to bring about a peaceful relationship between the Kauravas and our cousins. War has to be avoided if possible. If nothing comes of this peace mission there is always a war which will settle everything one way or the other."

War became inevitable. Preparations were in progress. The armies from all over Bharatavarsha were marching towards the banks of the river Ganga. Kings were taking sides in the war to come. Some were for Duryodhana and the others were coming to aid the Pandavas.

Duryodhana and Arjuna went to Swaraka to ask Krishna for his help. Both were in Dwaraka at almost the same time. When the Kaurava monarch arrived in the palace of Krishna he was told that Krishna was asleep. He strode into the sleeping chambers of Krishna. He saw a richly covered seat placed at the head of the bed and promptly he went and seated himself on it. A few moments later Arjuna entered the palace and he saw Duryodhana and he saw that Krishna was asleep. In all humility he sat at the foot of the bed and with folded hands waited for Krishna to wake up.

When Krishna opened his eyes, they rested on Arjuna. With a smile he welcomed Arjuna and then he saw Duryodhana. His greeting of Duryodhana was effusive and he spoke to them both with sweet words. Arjuna and the Kaurava monarch told Krishna about the reason for their hurrying to Swaraka. Each one asked Krishna to take sides with him. And Duryodhana said: "Krishna, I was here before Arjuna and it is but right that you should grant my request and not Arjuna's." Krishna said: "Of course, you are right. You came first. But then when I woke up from my sleep, I saw Arjuna first and I saw you after that. I am in a fix and so I will try and help you both."

Krishna paused for a moment and said: "Listen, there are two things to choose from. On the one hand I will be there, but I will be alone. I have sworn that I will not take up any weapon in this war. Krishna without a weapon: and on the other hand there will be an akshowhini of the Yadava army. Each warrior is as powerful as any one of my sons and they are all called the Narayanas. It is up to you both to choose either me, alone and weaponless, or the akshowhini. Arjuna is younger and so he should have the first choice."

Arjuna did not hesitate even for a moment. He said: "Krishna, I do not want your army. I want you and only you. Your blessings will steer me through my troubles. I choose you."

Duryodhana was happy to get the Yadava army of an akshowhini. The strength of this army was well-known.

He went to Balarama and told him about his getting the army. Balarama said: "Duryodhana, I am very fond of you. It is unfortunate that you have let slip the opportunity of getting Krishna on your side. As for me, I will not take sides in this war. Abandon the hope that I will come to your rescue. Under no provocation can I fight with my brother Krishna."

Krishna became the charioteer of Arjuna as he had sworn that he would not fight, and he led the Pandavas to their ultimate victory.

Negotiations for Peace

From Virata a Brahmin had been sent to Hastina. He arrived at the city and was taken to the court of the Kaurava king. He spoke to the elders there and to the old king Dhritarashtra about the message of the Pandavas. Vidura and Beeshma, who had great affection for the Pandavas, honored the Brahmin and spoke loving words of welcome. Everyone was eager to hear him speak. He spoke words which were soft and at the same time true.

He said: "The elders of the court should look kindly on me and listen to the words I have been asked to speak. It will be superfluous for me to say that great and wise men are here, men who are well-versed in the nuances of Dharma. They know what justice is and what is not. It will not be hard for them to understand what I am trying to communicate to them.

"The world knows that Pandu and Dhritarashtra are brothers and it follows that this kingdom belongs to both of them and, naturally, to their children. Why then is the share of the Pandavas denied to them? The sons of Dhritarashtra seem to be owning the entire kingdom. The Pandavas have been treated unfairly all through their lives. In the beginning attempts were made to kill them. Fortunately they were able to escape that. When that attempt proved futile, the game of dice was arranged and their kingdom was taken away from them. Draupadi was hurt and insulted in this same sabha and yet the Pandavas have borne all these patiently and they are willing to let bygones be bygones. They have completed the terms of the banishment and now they are asking for their share of the kingdom as per the conditions to which Duryodhana had agreed. Their demand is but just. If, however, Duryodhana is not willing to accede to their demand and if he desires war, he will certainly get what he is asking for. But the consequences of war are fearful and should be avoided if possible. The Pandavas are by no means weaklings. Krishna is with them and Dharma is with them. They have the assistance of great heroes who are willing to fight for them if the need arises. It will be of great benefit to the Kauravas if they accept the fact that the Pandavas should be given their share of the kingdom. I ask the elders here to convince Duryodhana that he should abandon this sinful avarice or else his unjust obstinacy will lead to his destruction.

"Either he should do so, or he should be prepared to be burnt in the fire of the anger of the Pandavas. I assure you, Duryodhana and all his associates will be burnt to ashes if he dares to challenge the fury of the Pandavas."

Bheeshma was listening to these words of the Brahman. He agreed with him and he said: "We know full well that Yudhishthira is a very righteous man and that he has been treated unjustly. What this messenger of the Pandavas says is but the truth. I am fully convinced that Yudhishthira is eager for peace and nothing else. His gentle reminder that he should get his kingdom back is right."

Karna got up even before Bheeshma could complete his words. He began to insult the old grandsire. Bheeshma was highly incensed by his words. There was a heated exchange and in the end Dhritarashtra managed to send the Brahmin back with the words: "I will discuss the matter with the elders here and I will send word to my dear nephew Yudhishthira with Sanjaya, my charioteer."

A few days later Sanjaya reached Upaplavya where the Pandavas were staying. The words he spoke were by no means pleasing to the Pandavas. The old king had sent a message which was full of Vedanta, with words which were insincere. Dhritarashtra had said: "Child Yudhishthira, you do not like violence and so I suggest that you should give up all thoughts of war. War is sinful and even if you do not get back your kingdom, you should not grieve. Never under any circumstance should a man resort to violence, forgetting the lesson of compassion. For the welfare of mankind, a human being should renounce all selfish thoughts. This is the ultimate Dharma. I have confidence in you: that you will listen to my words and make the others, Bhima and Arjuna, agree with me and Krishna too. Selflessness is the ultimate Dharma of every human being and I say that you should follow my suggestion: war should be averted; you should abandon this desire for a kingdom. Consider the lives which will be lost if there is a war. You should not be the cause of this bloodshed. Consider my words carefully. I know that you will listen to my advice."

Steeped as he was in thoughts of peace and gentleness, Yudhishthira found these words of his uncle to be too full of hypocrisy to be accepted. He became extremely angry and said: "Sanjaya, it is evident that the avarice in the mind of my uncle has prompted him to speak these words and send this message of 'peace' to me. He is but repeating what his dear son feels. You know only too well how I hate the thought of war. All I am asking for is justice. But the king has never once thought rightly. He has always had an inclination to favor Adharma. When the game of dice was progressing he knew that it was wrong, that they were deliberately cheating me and yet he spoke not a word to his son to stop the game. He did not lift up a little finger. During the entire game only two words were escaping his lips: 'Who won?' He was keen that Duryodhana should win and he completely disregarded thoughts of Dharma and Adharma.

"The insult to Draupadi was also countenanced by him calmly. He seemed to sanction every sinful action of his sons. Duryodhana at least is frank in his dealings with me now. He has said clearly that he will not give me back my kingdom. But this uncle of mine is a hypocrite. He has no intention of giving me anything and he has absolutely no feelings of compassion as far as our sufferings are concerned. He is indifferent to the fact that he is an Adharmi. He does not want to think of justice. And yet he has the audacity to teach me Vedanta: the lesson of renunciation. Go back to my uncle and tell him: 'Yudhishthira wants nothing but peace. The Pandavas have never once swerved from the path of Dharma. But we demand that justice is meted out to us. Give me back my kingdom and Intraprastha. This demand is not wrong as the kingdom belongs to me by right. Convey the message to my uncle that Yudhishthira wants his kingdom and if he is not denied his rights there will be no war'."

Sanjaya intervened and said: "You have not heard the entire injunctions of your uncle. The king has also said: 'Man's life on this earth is very short. In this short span why do you long so much for a transient and short-lived pleasure? Because of this you want to kill your own kinsmen in a dreadful war. Why do you want to commit this sin? The world will condemn your actions and you will only win their censure. Infamy will cling to your name. You will spend the rest of your life in pain and unhappiness as the burden of this sin will rest heavily on your shoulders. Give up this thirst for kingdom and forget all about a war with your cousins. It is not fitting that you should let this desire for a kingdom gain ascendance over you. It is a fleeting pleasure and a wise man like you should realize that it is so. You have spent thirteen years of your life in the forests and you were very brave about it. Continue to have the same fortitude and give up this wish to fight with us. You are approaching your old age and death is near at hand. Why this wish to rule a kingdom? Turn your thoughts away from such transient pleasures.

"You had no desire to fight during these thirteen years and you were patient and noble. Because you behaved as you did, we were under the impression that you would forget everything. But it is not so. You seem to be trying to reopen old wounds and make them bleed again. Wise men, I know, try to coax others from fighting, but you seem to have taken leave of your senses since you talk of war.

"Anger is the greatest poison which sullies the mind of man and a man who becomes a slave to anger is not wise. This is why the really good men swallow their anger and attain peace. There is a possibility that you may make up your mind to kill your grandfather Bheeshma, Drona and all my sons. Tell me, what do you hope to gain by this wholesale massacre? I am certain that even if you are the victor, and after the death of all your kinsmen, you will spend the rest of your life repenting the action which you once felt was right. Your entire life after the war will be full of sorrow. And so I am telling you once again, renounce anger. Go back to the forest. You should spend your time with a beggar's bowl and I am sure the Yadavas will take care of you. The rest of your life will be full of peace."

Sanjaya sat silent after speaking these words. For a long moment the Pandavas were silent. They were too stunned to talk. Even Bhima could not speak. And then all the brothers spoke impassioned words. Arjuna said: "Let us march now, at once, towards Hastina and begin the war."

Yudhishthira turned to Sanjaya and said: "Sanjaya, my uncle is an elder and he has a right to speak about my 'welfare'. But he is misusing the power he has over me as an elder. Krishna will reply to this message from the old king. Whether I intend to fight or give up all thoughts of fighting rests entirely on the wisdom of Krishna. I can do nothing, absolutely nothing, without the approbation of Krishna. As long as Krishna is by my side I have no worries. Nothing can upset me. Krishna, you tell me, what do you think of this message from my uncle?"

Krishna was touched by the words of Yudhishthira and he spoke to him: "Sanjaya, my first duty is to the Pandavas. I have their welfare in my mind always. And, at the same time, I wish that the sons of Dhritarashtra should be long-lived. I am not able to take the words of the old king calmly. He knows only too well that Yudhishthira is in the right and that his sons have done these brothers a grave injustice. But he seems to accuse Yudhisthira of selfishness! You know, Sanjaya, about the attitude of Yudhishthira towards Dharma. To him it is a religion. Dharma should be followed at any cost is the rule he has always followed. He spent these thirteen years with great courage and patience because he was bent on following the path of Dharma. He could easily have precipitated a war as soon as the banishment was pronounced. The game was unfair and the terms of the banishment were unfair and yet, because of his reverence for Dharma, he refrained from giving vent to his anger and bore the years of banishment. And yet the Kaurava king Dhritarashtra dares to accuse him of selfishness and this is clear proof that the old man has lost his senses completely. He has no right to talk about Vedanta to his nephew. He is arrogant and he is proud. Listen, Darupadi was insulted and for that one sin the entire Kaurava clan deserves to be wiped out. We can never forget that incident even for a moment. It is always throbbing in our minds like a wound which leaves a scar behind. When they left for the forest Bhima took an oath and he has not forgotten it. Dusshansana laughed at Bhima and called him 'Cow'. Bhima has not forgotten that either, and he is bent on keeping his word: he will surely drink the blood of Dusshasana. Tell Duryodhana that even in his dreams there is but one thought in the mind of Bhima: the breaking of the thighs of that sinner. He will certainly do it. You know all these things, Sanjaya. You could not have forgotten the events of those days so soon. How then could your kind have wiped them clean from his mind? If, however, he has forgotten them, I will come and remind him; I will recount each incident vividly and he is sure to wince at my words.

"And yet, we are for peace. Go and tell your king that I will come to Hastina and I will try to talk to his sons. I will make every attempt to convince them that they should return his kingdom to Yudhishthira and thus avert the war. If, however, they still refuse to listen to my words, there is a certain cure for their arrogance and avarice: the sharp arrows which are lying sleeping in the quivers of Arjuna. If Duryodhana is wise and accepts my advice then there need be no talk of war, and peace will become the heritage of all. I will take the entire responsiblity to see that there is no war."

Sanjaya made preparations to return to Hastina. He took leave of the Pandavas. When he was on the point of leaving, he said: "Yudhishthira, remember that I have great affection for you and you must consider me as your friend and well-wisher. The words I spoke are the words of your uncle and not mine. I am but the messenger sent by the king. It pains me that I had to speak these words to you and they have hurt you so. I am sorry."

Yudhishthira waived his apology aside and then spoke words which expressed his wish for the well-being of his uncle and his sons. Arjuna was not pleased at all by the gentleness with which he spoke. His words were harsh and he asked Sanjaya to repeat them to Duryodhana. Yudhishthira, however, would not give up his nature and he again asked in soft words that he should get back Indraprastha and his kingdom.

Sanjaya went back to Hastina and went straight to the palace where the old king was wont to stay. Dhritarashtra was waiting impatiently for the coming of Sanjaya to know what had taken place at Upaplavya. Sanjaya spoke sharply and his words were terse: "Yudhishthira sends his salutations to you. He wanted to know about the welfare of each and every one of you. The Pandavas are well and they have Krishna with them. During the few days I spent there, I was very happy. The atmosphere there is so clean, so pure and peaceful. My mind was reveling in this respite. Here the very air around you is full of sin, it is unclean. I do not relish either your behavior or your words. I was sent as a messenger and I did my duty as a Duta, an envoy, but I was not happy to do it. You are addicted only to sin and yet you seem to wish for nothing but good to happen to you. I am surprised at your optimism. I gave them your 'message'. As for the reply given by the noble Yudhishthira, I will talk to you about it tomorrow. I am very tired and I need to rest."

Sanjaya went away from his presence abruptly. The old blind king was greatly upset. His mind was filled with misgivings and the night was spent without sleep. Try as he might, sleep refused to visit his eyes and he sent for Vidura. When he came, the king said: "Vidura, I am very much upset. I am not able to sleep. Speak to me words which may grant me some peace of mind."

Vidura then spoke to him about many things. He gave a lengthy discourse on Dharma and this is famed as "Vidura-Neeti". He talked to the old king about Dharma, about how the king was straying from it and he advised him to restrain Duryodhana and his brothers. But it was of no use.

The next day Sanjaya spoke in detail about the events which took place in Upaplavya: about his message and the reaction of the Pandavas and of Krishna. He spoke in the assembly hall where everyone had gathered to hear him. After he had finished talking, silence pervaded the entire hall. Bheeshma, who was very fond of Duryodhana, tried to talk to him gently and make him listen to the words of advice given by all of them. He wanted to save all of them and he suggested that Duryodhana should agree to the demands of the Pandavas and return their kingdom to them. But it was a futile attempt.

Karna did not like this advice from the old man and he spoke harsh words, but the old man paid no heed to him. He continued to talk to Duryodhana, ignoring Karna's outburst. But the proud prince would not speak a word in reply. As for the old king he asked Sanjaya again and again to repeat all the words spoken at Upaplavya. Sanjaya spoke about the prowess of the Pandanvas, and while talking, he was so overcome with emotion that he fell down in a dead faint. Dhritarashtra's heart was full of fear. The future appeared to him in a dreadful form. It was like the great fire at the end of the yuga when everything is caught in the great conflagration and when sheets of flame envelop the entire world. And he wailed: "Sanjaya, what am I to do? My sons will not pay heed to my words."

Sanjaya could not keep silent and he said: "O king, actually the sin is yours. You would never pay any attention to the words of elders like Bheeshma, Vidura and others. When the game of dice was being played, I was there and I was watching you. All the time you were wishing that your son should win. And now your son will surely be destroyed. But he and his brothers will have the good fortune to die on the battlefield. But, the sinner that you are, you will be denied even that privilege. You will hear about the death, the annihilation of your entire family, and you will have to live after that. I am very sorry for you."

Sanjaya and Vidura and the others tried again to make Duryodhana understand the seriousness of the situation and to make him agree to the proposals for peace. Duryodhana sat listening to them for a while. His anger was rising and finally, he stamped out of the hall in a fit of fury.

Dharma and Adharma

Krishna had sent word to Dhritarashtra through Sanjaya that he would be in Hastina with a view to bring about peace between the Pandavas and Duryodhana. He had said that he would try his best to avert a war which could cause the end of the entire clan. Accordingly, Krishna made preparations to visit Hastina.

It was necessary to find out the feelings in the minds of each one of the brothers before he left and he sat with them discussing his proposed visit to Hastina. He asked them one by one what they thought of his mission. Yudhishthira was the first to speak. He said: "It is very necessary that you should go to Hastina at the moment. Dhritarashtra, as we know, has lost all sense of fairness of Dharma and this inner blindness in him cannot be cured. I am only sorry that I have been born as a Kshatriya, Krishna. I am therefore compelled to talk of war. If I had not been a Kshatriya, but were a Sudra, I could make a living out of serving others. If I had been a Vaishya, that profession would have given me enough to make a living. If I had been a Brahmin, a begging bowl would have been sufficient to serve my needs. But I am a Kshatriya born in the noble line of the Moon. It is the rule that a Kshatriya has a right only to give and never to ask for alms. And because of the avarice of my old uncle, I have been forced to think of war. I will have to watch the death of my kinsmen, of those who were once dear to me. If I refrain from fighting, infamy will be my heritage and I will be the object of ridicule. This is why I beseech you, Krishna, to try and avert the war. I am happy that you have offered to make every attempt to see that there is no war. It is a commendable task you have undertaken and I have great faith in you. I have hopes that you will succeed where others have failed."

Krishna said: "I will do my very best to convince them about the need for peace and if I succeed, then thousands of lives will be saved."

Yudhishthira added: "Krishna, I am afraid to send you to the Kaurava court. That sinful Duryodhana may try to harm you."

Krishna smiled and said: "I grant that Duryodhana is a sinner and he is capable of anything nefarious so long as it serves his purpose. But rest assured, Yudhishthira, that he cannot harm me. If, however, he does attempt some such foolishness, then, before you even think of a war, I would have destroyed him and his entire clan. Do not worry about me. But I have a feeling that this mission of mine will be fruitless. I have no hopes of bringing about peace.

"Sanjaya told you the views which the old man has about the entire situation. After that, you should not, even for a moment, think kindly of the Kauravas. No mercy should be shown to them. You are a Kshatriya and there are only two paths open to a Kshatriya. It is either victory or death. Both of these should be welcomed with open arms by a Kshatriya. Do not show signs of relenting, of weakening, in your words. In your affection for your kinsmen, you are apt to turn your face away from war. Do not give in to this cowardice. The Kauravas are sinners and they deserve to be killed.

"A Kshatriya has no kinsmen. You will have to be firm and forget the affection you have for the grand old man Bheeshma who is your grandfather.

"The vital question has to be weighed: which is to be victorious, Dharma or Adharma? There is no thought here of kinsmen or strangers. When Adharma was reigning supreme in the court of the old king neither Bheeshma nor Drona made any attempt to cry a halt and to reprimand Duryodhana. Draupadi was insulted and even then, even when a woman's honor was threatened, these elders sat silent. They will have to be punished for their countenancing Adharma. They have themselves been Adharmis. They will all have to taste the punishment for tolerating such Adharma. The court of the Kauravas is a hotbed of sin and it is but right that everyone there should be destroyed. I know that I will not succeed in this 'Mission of Peace' on which I have offered to go. You may wonder why I am going even when I know what is to happen there. I am going because I want to let the citizens of Hastina know about the tyranny of Duryodhana, their king, and about the path of Dharma which you have always followed. I want the world to know about it. I will go now. During my absence, please hurry with the preparations for the war which, I know, is inevitable."

Krishna turned his eyes to Bhima and waited for him to speak. With his face downcast, with a soft voice, Bhima said: "Krishna, I will be happy if you succeed in your attempts at peace. I know that Duryodhana is a sinner and insufferably arrogant. Still, I vote for peace."

Krishna laughed loudly and said: "Bhima, such gentleness, such humility, such desire for 'Peace'! When did these three come into being in your mind, Bhima? Till as recently as yesterday you were talking excitedly about the war to come and today you talk about peace and how good it will be for all. All these thirteen years were years which you spent with great difficulty and not a single night have you slept in peace because your dreams were haunted by thoughts of revenge on these sinners, which you had sworn. Again and again you would remind yourself of the oaths you have taken. And now, suddenly, you seem to have become a lover of peace! You are a Kshatriya, Bhima, and I am telling you: remember the sins of the Kauravas. So long as they are alive you will have no peace."

Bhima was touched to the quick by Krishna's words. He said: "Krishna, do you think I am a weakling? Is that why you are heaping insults on me? I am the same old Bhima and nothing can change me and my feelings."

"Prepare yourself, Bhima," said Krishna. "The war is imminent and nothing can avert it."

Arjuna was calm and smiling when Krishna looked at him. He said: "I am not worried about anything. Do what you think is best under the circumstances. If there is to be a war, we are prepared for it; if there is to be no war, it will be good for all. Everything is in your hands."

Krishna said: "Arjuna, remember, time is the most powerful factor that should be considered. What has been ordained by the fates cnannot be altered by human efforts. You know this truth. If you think that I am capable of doing anything I please, it is wrong. I am not a god and I let things happen the way they have been destined to happen."

Nakula and Sahadeva gave their opinions and they were very emotional about it. Satyaki was furious and he said: "Krishna, only death can cure Duryodhana of his sinful nature."

It was Draupadi's turn. Krishna turned his eyes slowly towards her. She was silent all this while but, when Krishna looked at her, tears sprang to her eyes. She held her long flowing tresses in her hand and said: "Krishna, do you remember? When that sinner Dusshasana touched these tresses of mine, they become unclean and since that moment I have not dressed them or bound them up. It is only when the arm of Dusshasana is fallen on the ground that I can find a semblance of peace. Anger is burning me up day and night and only you can grant me peace." Tears choked her and she could speak no more.

Krishna said: "Draupadi, do not weep. In a few days you will see the tears of the queens of these sinners."

Krishna took leave of them all and turned his chariot towards Hastina. Satyaki went with him.

The spies in the Kaurava court told the king about the journey of Krishna, that he had left Upaplavya for Hastina. There was a hurried summons sent to everyone and the court assembled for discussions. Bheeshma, Drona, and Vidura were there and Sanjaya was asked to be present. Dhritarashtra said: "Krishna is coming to Hastina with a desire to avert the war which is in the mind of everyone. Krishna is a great man and we should make every attempt to make his visit comfortable. He should be pleased with us and it is essential that he should be favorably inclined towards us. I suggest that steps be taken at once to provide him with comfort of every sort during his journey to Hastina."

He turned to Duryodhana and said: "Duryodhana, if we manage to please Krishna and win his favor it will be of immense value to us. I wish to know what my grandfather thinks of this suggestion of mine."

Bheeshma accepted the suggestion and Duryodhana said: "So be it. I will see to the arrangements for the comfort of Krishna."

Dhritarashtra then turned to Vidura and said: "Krishna will arrive in Kushasthala tonight and tomorrow he will be in Hastina. Vidura, you should see to all the arrangements to welcome this great soul to our city.

"Gifts of jewels, precious stones and pearls of immense value should be given to our honored guest. A beautiful chariot, to which are yoked noble horses, should be at the disposal of Krishna. Innumerable gifts should be showered on him so that he will be overwhelmed. I am eager to placate him. Am I not right in my surmise that these are good plans?"

Vidura smiled a slight, dry smile and said: "Never before has been born on this earth a great man like Krishna and such a being will not be born again in the near future. And you talk like a child about this man. You do not know Krishna. You seem to be under the impression that he can be bought over by meagre gifts like pearls and gems. How stupid you are. I cannot help laughing at your foolishness. All of a sudden you have become so generous with gifts; it is really surprising to me! You are not prepared to give even five villages to the Pandavas and yet you are ready to shower Krishna with gifts. If you really wish to please Krishna, there is but one way to do it. Accept his proposals for peace. Listen to him and do what he suggests. The greatest honor to Krishna will be paid by you if you treat his words with respect and act accordingly. He is coming here because he wishes you well. He wants peace. Do not make me laugh by suggesting that we should win him over with gems and pearls. I am still amazed at your sudden generosity!"

Duryodhana was listening to the words of Vidura, and he said: "I agree with uncle Vidura. He is saying what is true. Krishna's affection for the Pandavas is well known. Your idea is foolish. Krishna is not such a fool as to be trapped by the stupid web of bribery which you are spinning. It is an insult to Krishna even to think that you can tempt him as you are trying to. Krishna is the greatest of the great. He is certainly to be welcomed with all honor, but please forget these thoughts of pleasing him with gifts. It is not right. It is sheer lunacy to think of it."

Bheeshma said: "Krishna is far above praise or insults. He is a sublime personage and, as Vidura said, the only manner in which we can please him is to treat his suggestions with respect and listen to them."

Duryodhana was not quite pleased with the words of Bheeshma. He said: "Grandfather, according to you, only the Pandavas are righteous and you are never tired of praising them. But I have planned something. I am going to capture Krishna and imprison him. The Pandavas will be helpless without him and the entire issue will be solved easily. This seems to me to be the best course to adopt and I will adopt it."

Dhritarashtra was taken aback by these words and he said: "My son, do not do such a foolish thing. Krishna has come as a Duta and he is related to us. It is sinful to think of harming him. Give up this thought, my child."

Bheeshma sprang up from his seat in sheer disgust and said: "Dhritarashtra, you are doomed. Your son is bent upon destruction and he will achieve it, I know. I am sick of listening to his words. I do not want to hear any more. Just let me go away from here."

Bheeshma walked away out of the hall with angry strides.

Duryodhana—an Adharmi

Krishna arrived in Hastina. All the elders of the royal house went to receive him—Bheeshma, Drona, Kripa and others. Duryodhana was there with his brothers and Karna. The entire city was excited at the thought that Krishna had come to Hastina. Krishna was taken to the palace of Dhritarashtra. He was offered a jeweled seat. He was smiling and accepted the affection shown him by the others. He saluted the elders and spoke the conventional words of greetings and then left the palace. He went straight to the house of Vidura. He met Kunti, the mother of the Pandavas. After the exchange of preliminaries, Krishna said: "My dear aunt, your days of pain are drawing to an end. The rays of happiness are just appearing on the horizon. Soon, very soon, the Pandavas will be rewarded for their fortitude. Shed your worries and be happy."

Krishna then went to the palace of Duryodhana. It was a magnificent palace and could easily compare with Indra's home in the heavens. Krishna ascended the steps and arrived in the courtyard of the king's house. Duryodhana was there on a throne surrounded by his courtiers.

As soon as Krishna entered, they all stood up as one man—Duryodhana, Sakuni, Dusshasana, Karna and others. They welcomed with him with courtesy and offered him a gorgeous seat. It was carved out of ivory and inlaid with gold and gems.

A smile lit up the face of Krishna. After a while Duryodhana said: "Krishna, I am grieved because you refused our hospitality. I had made such elaborate preparations to entertain you. We had prepared a wonderful feast for you, But you ignored all that and went to the house of Vidura. This has pained me and all of us."

Krishna listened to him and then said: "Duryodhana, why do you take it to heart? You have welcomed me really with great affection and show of courtesy. This complaint of yours is needless. After my mission is over, I will remain in your house and I will willingly accept your hospitality."

Duryodhana said: "That is beside the point. The mission has nothing to do with the fact that you are our cousin. You are as dear to us and near to us as you are to the Pandavas. I was hoping that you would be my guest and I was eager to play host to you. There has been no conflict between me and you, but you chose to ignore me and that has hurt me."

Krishna said: "As you seem to make an issue of it, I will explain why I did this. I do not relish food in this house. I am not impressed by all these preparations to entertain me. I will be happy to partake of the food only in a house where truth and righteousness dwell always. As for you, you hate the Pandavas. This hatred is intense. This is an unreasonable feeling and there is no grounds for it. When a man becomes a slave to his feelings, when he gives in to the sin of avarice and forgets what is right and what is not, he is considered to be the lowliest of the low by me. To me, the food in your house will be the food in the house of an enemy. How can I eat it? The Pandavas happen to be my very life because they have always been following the path of truth. This is the reason why I avoided your hospitality. Vidura is a good man and he is righteous and so I went to his house. You have forced me to tell you the truth."

Krishna got up from his seat and walked away from there. He did not wait for the chariot but went on foot to Vidura's house.

Bheeshma and Kripa went with him. Bheeshma said: "We have prepared a mansion for your stay. Come, let us go there."

Krishna shook his head and said: "My lord, you have

blessed me and that is hospitality enough as far as I am concerned. Forgive me for my choosing Vidura's house. Please go back to your mansions as I will not stir out of Vidura's house."

He was welcomed with great affection by Vidura. After he had eaten, Krishna and Vidura conversed about the subject which was uppermost in their minds. Vidura said: "Krishna, your coming is a waste. Duryodhana is a fool and obstinate too. He is convinced that he is going to win this war. Bheeshma, Drona, Kripacharya, Ashvatthama, Karna and Jayadratha are the heroes on whom he is depending and he has at his command an immense army. He says again and again: 'Karna can, single-handed, destroy the entire Pandava host.' How will it be possible to bring him to his senses? He is bent on war."

Krishna was listening silently while Vidura went on: "Krishna, I am not happy at the thought of your sitting in their midst even. I do not advise you to go to the palace of Dhritarashtra. They are sure to insult you. They are even capable of harming you. I am greatly worried for you."

Krishna said: "Vidura, I know that you are my well-wisher. I know that all this is true. Knowing it, I have come here as I want to escape the censure of the world. I want to rescue the world from the jaws of death. If I am able to achieve my purpose, it will be well. If I do not, I will have the satisfaction of knowing that I did make an attempt to save the world.

"Vidura, if a man thinks sinful thoughts and does not translate them into action, he is saved from the punishment for the sin. And so, I say, if I am able to prevent these two sinners, the father and son, from doing anything sinful, I will then be saving them from destruction.

"A great disaster is threatening the House of the Kurus. Clouds of destruction have gathered in the heavens. If a man sees that someone is in danger and does not make an attempt to save him from that danger, then the watcher is not a man but an animal. The sinner may be heading for his own end, but it is the duty of a good man to drag him forcibly, if necessary, from the abyss towards which he is heading. That is why I am here. Mine is an attempt to save mankind. Therefore, I will try to convince Duryodhana that Yudhishthira wants peace and only peace. The Pandavas are dear to me. Yudhisthira is a great soul. He is the image of Dharma and I am proud to know that he has great faith in me. He loves me and I am proud of the fact. I wish to please him and so I have taken up this seemingly impossible task.

"There is another word to be spoken in this context. I will speak words which will convince the entire world that Yudhishthira was averse to war: that he wanted to make peace with Duryodhana and it was the Kaurava king who chose to fight with the Pandavas. The world should know, men in aftertimes should know, the truth. They should know the difference between these two men: the one who will not swerve from the path of Dharma and the other who does not know what Dharma is. I want the kings who are siding with the Kauravas to know where justice lies, where truth is to be found. They should realize that they are siding with a sinner. Bheeshma, Drona and the others in the court should be made to realize that they have a share in this ignominy. If, after all these attempts have failed, war takes place, then the world will know about Yudhishthira and his desperate efforts for peace. This, and only this, is the reason for my coming to Hastina on this fruitless mission."

The next day, early in the morning, Duryodhana came to the house of Vidura accompanied by Karna and others to take Krishna to the court. Daruka brought the chariot of Krishna and Krishna sat in it and he took Vidura with him. Duryodhana and Karna followed him in the royal chariot. Satyaki and Kritavarma followed them in another chariot.

A section of the Kaurava army was arrayed to honor Krishna's arrival at the court. The entire city was lining the streets to have a look at this great personage.

Holding the hands of Vidura and Satyaki, Krishna descended from his chariot. Duryodhana and Karna walked with him and, as he entered the palace, the elders stood up and the old king welcomed Krishna. A jeweled seat had been set apart for him. Just before he sat down Krishna saw that the divine rishis led by Narada had assembled there and were eager to enter the palace. Krishna indicated this to Bheeshma who hurried out to welcome the great sages. He was greatly excited at their coming.

They had all taken their seats and Krishna was seated too. A smile was lighting his face. Dusshasana led Satyaki to his seat and the brothers of Duryodhana made Kritavarma comfortable. Duryodhana and Karna were very near Krishna. And so was Sakuni. Vidura was glued to the side of Krishna.

All eyes were turned towards Krishna. They looked at him and they wanted to keep on looking. The magnetism of the man, the charm which was part of him, his fascinating smile, were making them experience a thrill which they had never known. The entire Sabha was glowing because of his presence. The jewel called Kaustubha was adorning his chest and he was dressed in his favorite yellow silk. It seemed as though the sun were rising from behind a dark mountain. There was nothing but silence in that great hall where they had all assembled to listen to the envoy of Yudhishthira.

Suddenly the silence was broken by the swan-like voice of Krishna. The very walls reverberated when his voice was raised, and it seemed like the echo of thunder which was roaring at a distance.

The Great Assembly

Krishna addressed Dhritarashtra and said: "Dhritarashtra, I have come here to save several of the great heroes of the world from the jaws of death." He paused for a moment to let his words make an impact and continued: "This is the sole reason why I have come to Hastina. My desire is to bring about peace between the Pandavas and the Kauravas. The noble line, of which you are a descendant, is famed all the world over. The House of the Kurus is the noblest House in the entire Bharatavarsha. Born as you are in such an illustrious line of kings, do you think it is right on your part to destroy this image?

"It is not fitting that you should behave thus. Your sons seem to have strayed from the path of Dharma long ago. They are pursuing this path of Adharma without a thought for the consequences. They do not seem to submit to discipline nor do they have any respect for the words of the elders. It is not as though you are unaware of their many ignoble acts. Things have now come to such a pass that the entire world is in danger.

"If you make up your mind, it is still possible for you to call them to order and make them tread the right path. Even if the task is hard it can be done if there is genuine desire to achieve it. And so, I am asking you to control the conduct of your sons and tell them what they should do. This entire court knows full well that this can be achieved if you exercise your power, your position as the king. Lead your sons away from the road to destruction. If you agree to a pact of peace between the Pandavas and your sons, then your fame will live for ever in the minds of men.

"Consider for a moment! If this were to happen, then you will have by your side your sons as well as the Pandavas and there will be no enemies to oppress you. No king will dare to try to fight with you because you will be protected by heroes, your sons and your brother's sons. Bheeshma, Drona and the others will be accompanied by Bhima and Arjuna, and is there any need for me to describe the glory that will be yours? This world and the *next* world will stand in awe of a powerful monarch like you. This entire world will be at your feet. Please let your mind dwell on this glorious picture.

"Instead of courting this fame and a great name, you are encouraging the sinfulness in your sons and you are busy winning the censure of the wise. What do you gain by seeing the breaking up of your family? Your sons will be killed and the heroes who have offered to stand by them will also be killed. Is this going to make you happy? Your son is powerful no doubt, but then the Pandavas are more powerful. The thought of war should be avoided since it will spell disaster to everyone. All the great warriors will meet with their deaths because of this war which can be avoided if you make up your mind. I appeal to you to do so.

"The Pandavas are good men. They have nothing but respect for you because you are the brother of their father. Go back some years, my lord, and think of the day when those fatherless children were brought to you and left under your care. They came to you seeking affection and protection but you did not treat them well. You were party to the plots to kill them. You allowed them to be banished to the forest and you have robbed them of their entire wealth and kingdom. This is sin.

"To wipe out the infamy which you have gained, you should change the course of action. Treat them as you would your children. Please walk away from the path of Adharma and save the world. You will then gain the love, respect and devotion of the Pandavas and you will have peace.

"This is a great opportunity which has come your way.

You can wash away all the many sins you have committed all these years. Give the Pandavas the love of a father and work for peace between the two factions.

"Tell me, where has Dharma gone? I do not find it in your court. Justice is suffocated and Truth is hidden away in the folds of untruth. The elders of the court sit still and do not raise a voice of protest when injustice is rampant. This is not a Sabha where Dharma can be found. This is a breeding place for Sin. It is not too late. Think of my words seriously and return their kingdom to the Pandavas.

"Yudhishthira is the very image of Dharma. He has been treated unjustly no doubt, but he will forget that and he will behave toward you as a son will toward his father. He will not bear any grudge toward you in his magnanimous heart. I can assure you of that.

"My lord, I am your well-wisher. I am thinking only of your welfare. This is why I want to rescue these sons of yours from certain death. If you want to spend your last days in peace then you should make peace with the Pandavas. There is no other way to assure you of a happy old age."

Krishna had stopped talking. Silence greeted his words. Everyone had been listening as though spellbound. The silence persisted for a long while and finally Dhritarashtra broke the silence.

He said: "Krishna, I have listened to your words with great care. But then, can you not see that I am helpless? There is no one here who will listen to my words. Duryodhana has no regard for me and he does not care to listen to me. If you are able to have some influence on him and Karna, if you can control them and their actions, I will be eternally grateful to you. Gandhari too has tried to talk to her son but she was also unable to move him. All these elders here, Bheeshma, Vidura and others, have not succeeded in making him see that it is an unwise path that he has adopted. I ask you to make an attempt and if you succeed there will be great relief and happiness in my mind."

Krishna turned his eyes to Duryodhana and began to talk to him. "Duryodhana," he said, "please listen to me. You are a scion of a noble House. You are intelligent and you have all the qualities which are the heritage of noble-born men.

How then could you think of stooping to these low acts? My dear Duryodhana, one born in a low house will have but low thoughts because he would have inherited them. It is only such men who will give in to feelings like envy and avarice. They will be mean and cruel because that is their nature. But you are different. The ancestry which you can boast of is different. Why do you act like a low-born man when you have the heritage of a long line of noble kings behind you? Only wicked men will resort to tactics like deceit and threat. By some unfortunate conspiracy of circumstances you seem to have forgotten your noble ancestry. This attitude will only make you an object of ridicule in the eyes of wise men. The infamy you are earning will cling to your name forever.

"I am asking you to heed my warning and set about the urgent task of saving your soul. There is still time. You can save yourself and your brothers. Turn your face away from the path you have been following all these many days. Try and consider the position intelligently. The wish of all the elders here and that of your father and mother is that you should opt for peace. It will be a gesture of nobility if you conform to their wishes and make them all happy. Why do you hesitate? Do not treat their words with so much indifference. They want you to live. Remember, Duryodhana, the only thing which will save you is peace between you and the Pandavas who have been ill-used till now.

"In the world, Duryodhana, there are to be found three types of men. There are those who are by nature righteous. The other type is the man who thinks only of himself and is selfish all the time. Even if you belong to this type of men, still it will be profitable for you to make peace with the Pandavas as it will be for your benefit. You have ambitions of being the lord of the world and you depend on Sakuni and Karna to help you realize this ambition. If you make friends with the Pandavas this will be made easy for you as these cousins of yours are powerful.

"Who is there in this world strong enough to face Bhima or Arjuna? Bheeshma, the veteran warrior of old, will himself be unable to face them. Make friends with the Pandavas and your father will be considered the monarch of this entire kingdom. No one can dare question his authority.

"I will tell you about the third class of men who are capable only of acting wrongly. They revel in sin and acts which are sinful. Without any reason they indulge in these. They lose sight of the fact that this will lead to their own destruction, and they pursue their sinfulness. I am sure you do not belong to this class of men!

"Think for a moment of the glory and grandeur that will be yours if you are at peace with the Pandavas! Why do you behave thus? Why are you blind to all the advantages of this peace? Come, wake up. Abandon this attitude and come out of this spiritual darkness. Let your mind be suffused with a new light, a new glow. Give them back their share of the kingdom and save mankind from destruction which is certain unless you avert it."

Krishna spoke clearly and one could see that he was sincere in his appeal to Duryodhana and his better nature. Dhritarashtra realized how evil his thinking had been. It was as though he had been hiding behind a curtain all these days and this was suddenly torn asunder and his atrocities exposed ruthlessly. Bheeshma and Drona and all the other elders were made to see their shortcomings. Even Duryodhana seemed to listen earnestly to the possibilities of a dread future if he persisted in his obstinate refusal. Krishna told him that there was hope for him still if he would only agree to the proposals laid before him. Krishna emphasized the fact that the reputation of the House of the Kurus was at stake and that it was the responsibility of the king to save it from infamy.

Dhritarashtra took refuge in saying that he was helpless and he said nothing more. Drona was, of course, greatly impressed by the words of Krishna, but the only person who could save the situation was Duryodhana. They looked to him and waited for him to speak.

Duryodhana's face was a study in rage. He was boiling over with anger. He had been keeping his temper under control with great difficulty while Krishna was talking. But now, when silence set in, when he saw that they were all waiting for him to reply, his anger spilled over. He turned to Krishna with his eyes red with wrath and said: "Krishna, I have heard all that you wanted to say. You seem to have joined the crowd of people who have been importuning me. My father, my mother, my grandfather, my uncle have all been saying these same things to me and you are but repeating what I have been hearing these many days. I am accused by all of you. Of what? I cannot understand what I have done that I should be treated as a culprit. I will recount to you what happened. We played a friendly game of dice and Yudhishthira happened to lose all that he possessed willingly. I am not to blame for his foolishness! Actually it was all returned to him by me. But he played again and lost. He accepted the conditions of the game and went to the forest. Why should I be blamed for it? I am not in the wrong! I have not tried to deceive Yudhishthira nor have I made any attempt to ruin him. He seems to be bent on fighting with me and I am prepared to accept his challenge. I am not afraid. Even if the heavenly host led by Indra comes to the aid of this cousin of mine, I am not afraid. I have great heroes like Bheeshma, Drona and Karna to fight for me. I am a kshatriya and I can fight. I know my dharma. If it is destined that I should die on the battlefield I am not afraid either. The gates of heaven will be wide open for heroes like me who die on the field fighting. I would rather die than bend my head to anyone, least of all Yudhisthira.

"Tell Yudhishthira that his ambition to regain Indraprastha will remain a dream. He has lost it and he will never get it back. Krishna, listen to me carefully and remember what I say. I have no intention of returning Indraprastha to him. Tell him that even the smallest piece of land which can be covered by the tip of a needle will not leave my hands to oblige the 'ill-used' Pandavas. This is my final decision, and firm and irrevocable it will remain. I will not return the kingdom to Yudhishthira. You can take this message back to him from me."

Conquer Your Senses

The hall resounded with the sudden laughter of Krishna. He had been listening to the words of Duryodhana and this was his reply. The wise could see that there was anger and sorrow in that laughter of his. The entire hall trembled with fear when they heard Krishna laugh. They had, so far, seen nothing but a smile lighting his face. They had seen him with anger on his brows, and they had seen him when he was very thoughtful. But this laughter which struck terror into their hearts was something they had never heard before. Krishna stood up and they looked at him. His eyes were red, but there was no indication of anger on his face.

Krishna spoke to Duryodhana and in a soft voice said: "Duryodhana, listen to my words now. I can see that you are eager to embrace death. So be it. Your wish will be granted in a few days. You will certainly meet with the death which you are evidently pining for. Be brave, my friend. You, and, because of you, your brothers, your kinsmen and your friends will all rush into the mouth of Death.

"You dare to ask me how you have wronged Yudhisthira! Are you not ashamed of yourself when you ask this of me? Do you think that this great sabha is entirely unaware of the injustice meted out to Yudhisthira? Do you think the world is ignorant of it? Is it possible to conceal from the world the fact that Sakuni played a game of deceit and robbed the Pandava prince of his kingdom? Your dear brother dragged their queen by her hair to this same sabha and tried to dishonor her. These same elders were present then too, and they were watching this dastardly act, and they sat silent without a word of protest escaping from their lips. Do you think it will be possible for the words you spoke then to be forgotten? The words spoken by you, by Sakuni, by Dusshasana and by Karna? You tried to engineer the death of the Pandavas at Varanavata by setting fire to their 'palace'. You fed Bhima with poison and you flung him into the waters filled with poisonous snakes. All these acts have been credited to you and your sinful associates and yet you have the courage to ask me: 'How have I wronged Yudhishthira?' Have you taken leave of your sense, Duryodhana? You must have, or else you would not have spoken these words. You are a sinner of the worst type and you are worthy of the contempt of good and wise men."

Dusshasana intervened and said: "Duryodhana, my dear brother, there seems to be a conspiracy thought up by the old men here, Bheeshma, Drona and your father, aided by this Krishna, to capture you and us along with you. We will be led towards the Pandava camp and we will be forced to make peace with them."

Like a king cobra rearing up suddenly from the ground, Duryodhana stood up and walked out of the sabha with angry strides.

As Duryodhana, the image of arrogance, of anger and pride, walked out of the sabha he seemed like a tiger which walks away from the midst of a herd of cows. His anger had reached the very utmost limit and he could not bear to hear any word of advice from anyone. With him walked out his brothers and Karna.

Bheeshma was watching the entire proceedings and this sudden exit of Duryodhana made him angry and sad too. He said: "You are right, Krishna. Their end has come. You must believe me when I tell you that I tried to reason with him. The end of these grandchildren of mine is certain and equally certain is the end of all the kshatriyas of Bharatavarsha. I can only say that Fate is the most powerful factor and no one can alter the ways of Fate."

Krishna said: "My lord, I am afraid I will have to tell you

that you are all responsible for this predicament. You have been allowing this misbehavior on the part of Duryodhana and now it has gone too far. If you wish to do so, you can imprison Duryodhana and his supporters. There is still time. You can bind this sinner Duryodhana and save mankind. When the atrocities of my uncle Kamsa became unbearable, I killed him. I had no pity in my heart for him and I have no regrets even now about what happened. I killed my uncle, my own mother's brother, for the welfare of the world.

"If you follow my advice, you will place these men in prison and make the Pandavas rule the land. By these men I mean Duryodhana, Dusshasana, Sakuni and Karna. If these four are made captives the world will be saved from the fate threatening it. It has been said in the sacred books that a single individual can be sacrificed for the sake of the family; the family, for the sake of the village; the village itself for the sake of the community, and one's entire belongings should be sacrificed for the welfare of one's soul. The only way to save the kshatriyas from total annihilation is to imprison these wicked men. Listen to my words and do what I suggest."

Dhritarashtra heard the words of Krishna and he was mortally scared. He called Vidura to his side and said: "Call my queen Gandhari to the court. We will try and see if we can, together, think of something. If we succeed, then perhaps, out of fear for us, my son may obey us. Gandhari is a wise woman and perhaps she will have some influence on her son. Perhaps he will listen to her."

The queen mother came and the king said: "Gandhari, your son has reached the very extreme of sinfulness. He refuses to listen to the words of the elders here. A great calamity is imminent. Try and see if you can talk to your son and make him see reason."

Gandhari asked Vidura to fetch Duryodhana. When he had gone, she told Dhritarashtra: "My lord, a king who is extremely avaricious has no right to rule the kingdom. The ambition of Duryodhana has now broken its banks, no doubt. But I must admit that your sin is greater than that of your son. You were lost in your son and you chose to ignore all rules of dharma in your desire to please him. You willingly allowed him to ill-treat the sons of Pandu and you assisted him in his schemes. And now, suddenly, you wish to prove that you have a right to command him and ask him to do what you say. This is well-nigh impossible.

"In spite of my protests, you surrendered the reins of the kingdom to him. You are now reaping what you sowed long ago. You sided with Duryodhana and you allowed injustice to the Pandavas. This was unbecoming to a righteous ruler. You will have to suffer for what you did. The consequences cannot be ignored or avoided."

Duryodhana entered the sabha as his mother had asked for him. His eyes were glowing like live coals. Gandhari called him to her side softly and said: "Child, please listen to my words. You should make yourself worthy of ruling this great land of the Kurus. If a man cannot control avarice, hatred, arrogance and pride which are lodged in his heart, he is not fit to rule the kingdom. One whose senses are not under his control has no right to rule over a country. From this point of view you are absolutely unfit to be a king because you are a slave to these emotions. If you cannot conquer these enemies which are lodged in you, how can you hope to gain ascendancy over the enemies from outside?

"These weaknesses of yours are your enemies. Hold them down first and then you can try and see if you can fight others. Sit by my side, child, and listen patiently to my words. I am your mother and I am the greatest well-wisher you can have. I love you and I want to protect you. You are the son born to me and you are my firstborn. When you were born evil omens were seen. But I ignored the message they had as I was certain that a son born of me would never stoop to Adharma. But I see now that you are a sinner and you are threatening to bring destruction to the entire House of Kurus. Please give up these ways, child.

"You may not know it but I know: Krishna and Arjuna are the great sages Narayana and Nara born again in this world of men. Do not antagonize them. You will not be able to defeat them because they are divine. I am certain that victory is where dharma is and dharma is not on your side. Only Arjuna and Krishna will taste of victory and not you. These two will destroy the world and they will be the cause of your death. And so, I ask you once again, forget this enmity with the Pandavas and make peace with them."

Dhritarashtra tried to add a few words of his to those of Gandhari. But Duryodhana was furious with all those assembled there and, without speaking a word, without even letting his mother know that he had heard her, he went away from there.

Duryodhana went straight to where Karna was, along with Sakuni and Dusshasana. He said: "Look, they have called my mother to the assembly hall and another attempt is being made to 'control' me and my Adharma. I am getting tired of all this. I am disgusted with the words which they spout for my benefit. The time has come when I should put an end to these so-called 'wellwishers' and their 'advice'. They have decided that the four of us should be captured and flung into prison. They will then invite that milk-faced Yudhishthira to rule the kingdom. Even my father has agreed to this conspiracy. All this is, of course, a product of the brain of Krishna. He is familiar with this kind of tactics. I ask you, why should we not anticipate their move and capture Krishna ourselves? We will imprison him. He is the cause of all this and we should hasten to do so."

The Cosmic Form of the Lord

Satyaki came to know of the plan of the sinful four to capture Krishna. He went to Kritavarma and said: "Listen, your friend and his crowd have planned to capture Krishna and to imprison him. Go quickly and collect your army. I will hurry to Krishna and tell him about this development." He rushed to the side of Krishna and quietly told him about what was planned by Duryodhana. Dhritarashtra heard it too, and Vidura.

Satyaki said: "My lord, indeed your son is wise. He is trying to tie up a raging fire with a silken scarf." He was silent after that.

Vidura was stunned when he heard Satyaki. He tried to imagine what was to happen. But Krishna seemed to be unaffected by the news. He asked everyone to be calm and said: "Why are you all worried? There is no need for it. It is not all that easy to bind me and imprison me." He turned to the old king and said: "Dhritarashtra, your son's conduct has reached the limit. The cup is full and it needs to be emptied."

Dhritarashtra was frightened out of his wits. He sent for his son once again and said: "You are sinking deeper and deeper into the mire of sin. I knew that you were sinful, but I had no idea that you would reach this limit. What is this foolish plan of yours? Krishna is a great soul. No one can harm him. Even the gods will not be able to hurt him or harm him. The sun may, perhaps, be caught in two hands; the earth may, perhaps, be lifted up and flung aside with ease; the passing breeze may, perhaps, be captured, but Krishna cannot be bound by you and your men."

Krishna had a smile on his face when he said: "You fool! You seem to be under the impression that I am alone. I feel sorry for you. Just turn your eyes around you and look." Suddenly the sabha was packed. There were to be seen the Pandavas, the Andhakas, the Vrishnis, and the seven Maruts, the eleven Rudras, the eight Vasus and the twelve Adityas.

Krishna laughed loudly and out of his mouth emanated an unearthly glow. His body was glowing too. His form had changed. On his forehead could be seen Brahma and on his chest were to be seen the eleven Rudras. On his shoulders were to be seen Indra, Yama, Varuna and Kubera. They saw in his body the Adityas, the Vasus, the Ashvini twins, and on his left were arrayed the Pandava host. Out of his left hand Balarama could be seen emerging. To his right was stationed Arjuna with the Gandiva in his hand. Bhima, Nakula, Sahadeva and Yudhishthira were behind him. Warriors surrounded the Pandavas. Krishna seemed to have thousands of arms, and the conch, the disc, the mace and the lotus could be seen in his hands. Out of his eyes and his nose could be seen flames emerging. It seemed as though Death, which is considered to have no form, had assumed a frightening form and had come to visit them. Looking at the form before them the people in the sabha could not bear the glow and they closed their eyes. Only some were able to see him. Bheeshma, Drona, and the rishis assembled there were able to keep their eyes open and they looked at him as though they wished to drink him with their eyes. The Lord, in his infinite mercy, had granted them power enough to look on this form of his with their naked eyes.

A miracle was to be seen. Dhritarashtra, who was blind ever since he was born, was able to see the Vishvaroopa of the Lord since he was granted this privilege. His eyes now had life in them and he could see the Lord and His cosmic form. Music was heard from the heavens and flowers rained on the glorious form of the Lord. Tears were flowing from the eyes of Dhritarashtra and he said: "Krishna, you are the Lord of this Universe. It has been my good fortune that I could see this form of yours. After seeing this I do not desire that my eyes should see ordinary, mundane things. Please take back the sight which you have granted me."

The earth was quaking after the Vishvaroopa was seen. The ocean and the rivers were threatening to dry up. There was nothing but terror in the hearts of men. Krishna saw this and he withdrew the glorious form into himself and assumed his old smiling stature once again.

Krishna took leave of everyone. They led him to his chariot and he was silent. He spoke not a word to any of them. His eyes were full of misery. When he was leaving Dhritarashtra said: "Krishna, you saw for yourself how helpless I am. Please do not be angry with me. I do not hate the Pandavas. But I have no power over my son."

While he prepared himself to climb into the chariot Krishna said: "You have all seen how hard I tried to avert the war and to bring about peace between the cousins. You have also been witness to the arrogance of Duryodhana and his pride and his attempt to capture me, a Duta. I am going back without being able to achieve what I set out to do, because of this obstinate son of the king. I tried all methods but in vain. In aftertimes no one can say that Krishna did not make any attempt to avert the war. I am sorry I failed in my mission but I am glad that I made a sincere attempt."

Krishna went to the house of Vidura and he was soon with Kunti. He asked her: "I am going back. My dear aunt, what message have you for your sons?"

Kunti said: "Krishna, I am all eagerness to see my sons. But now tell them this: 'My sons, you are kshatriyas and you are the sons of Kunti. You have been blessed by the gods. All I ask is that you should do your duty as kshatriyas.' Tell Draupadi: 'I have been fortunate in having you as my son's wife. I am very pleased with you. Krishna will be there to protect you and I am not worried about the welfare of any of you. I bless you.'"

After Krishna had gone, there was another feeble attempt by Bheeshma and the others to talk Duryodhana out of his decision to make war with the Pandavas. Finally preparations had to be made for war.

The Mahabharata is full of the activities of Krishna. But

the most impressive, the most ennobling incident of them all is the role he played as the ambassador to the court of Duryodhana. His absolute mastery of statecraft, his words full of meaning, the skill with which he could lay bare the absolute truth about the feelings in the mind of each one there, his talk on justice, dharma and conduct, his attempt to coax the Kauravas to make peace with the Pandavas, his desire to avert the war, are all so wonderful that one can say without hesitation that all the politicians of today can easily learn from Krishna the art of diplomacy and statesmanship.

Krishna was partial to the Pandavas. He had no love for Duryodhana. Still, he was so broadminded that he tried to save Duryodhana and his evil mentors from destruction. This was the reason why he went to Hastina.

Krishna avoided the hospitality of Duryodhana. When he was compelled to give his reasons for this, he had to tell him: "So long as my task is unfinished, so long as the war which is looming ahead is not averted, I cannot be your guest. Once a decision is reached then it will be clear whether you are my friend or my enemy." Krishna did not believe in covering up truth with dubious words.

Krishna knew well that Duryodhana was capable of trying to harm him. But he was not afraid. He faced the situation with unbelievable courage and this was an unearthly feat. When he spoke to them he did not spare any of them: not Bheeshma nor Drona nor the old king. A man of such immense power and intellectual superiority is rarely to be found.

Krishna's wisdom, his dexterity with words, his courage, or rather, his fearlessness, his dedication to dharma, and his intellect which was as sharp as the edge of a sword, are all to be admired. It is amazing that one person could be the storehouse of all these many qualities.

The news that there was an attempt to imprison him did not perturb him in the least. He smiled at Satyaki and said: "Why! Are you afraid for me? It will not be an easy task to bind me. I am not alone! Not by any means!"

When he said that he was not alone Krishna meant not only the power of his arms but he spoke of the strength of dharma which was with him always. He had the strength of wisdom. It was Brahmatejas because he was a Brahmavit. It was because of this that Krishna was able to amaze the entire hall with his Vishvaroopa, to illumine it like the sun illumines the heavens. The entire heavenly host as well as that of the earth could be seen in that form which he had assumed.

It is immaterial here whether this form was seen by the earthly eyes of those around him or by the power of the "inner eye" as it is called. The effect was profound: the men in the enemy camp were frightened at the sight while the others felt a wave of faith sweep over them.

We must consider this phenomenon from the spiritual angle, which is the right approach. This entire episode holds a lesson for us. It teaches us the truth that the power of one's dharma, one's integrity, is greater than mere physical strength. This is the core of the Vishvaroopa chapter. We should try and gather the allegorical meaning of this. Everyone could not see the Vishvaroopa but only the gifted few. This means that those whose intellect had become dimmed by their departure from the path of dharma had lost their power to see Truth and they could not see this vision. They could not understand the underlying meaning of this manifestation: the truth that the entire Universe is but the Brahman, and Krishna was the Brahman as he was a Brahmavit.

Bheeshma and the others who saw the Visvaroopa were the intellectuals and they were able to see truth. The Lord gave the power of seeing with the "inner eye" to Dhritarashtra, which means that he could use his thinking if he would. A chance was given to him, but he was so frightened to face the truth that he wailed: "Please let me be without this power to see! I do not want to possess it. I have seen you once and I want nothing else."

This is the truth underlying the Vishvaroopa. The man endowed with the spiritual eye can see the great vision. The man in quest of truth must be equipped with the required frame of mind to face Truth when he gets a chance to see it: realization of the truth is not easy and it is given but to a few.

"This War Is a Yagna"

An incident occurred which reveals to us the real truth about Karna and his character. Some people have the wrong impression about Karna. He was the dearest friend of Duryodhana and so near were the two that the readers of the Mahabharata invariably bracket him with sinners like Sakuni and Dusshasana. He is also considered to be one of the "Sinful Four". That he was wicked and cruel like the others is an impression which has been created and his name has earned calumny because of his association with Duryodhana.

Vyasa has taken pains to reveal him to us as he really was. He has not placed him in the same class as the others. He has revealed to us that Karna, in spite of his being the dearest friend of Duryodhana, in spite of his being part of all the many dastardly actions of the Kauravas against the Pandavas, was, in reality, a great character. His nature was noble and his generosity and his love of dharma could not find an equal in the three worlds. Except that he was with Duryodhana, there could be no fault to be found in Karna.

The incident which reveals the character of Karna occurred after the visit of Krishna to the court of the Kauravas. When he had come out of the Hall, Krishna made preparations to return to Upaplavya. While he was about it, he called Karna to his side and asked him to sit with him in his chariot. Having a great regard for Krishna, Karna spoke not a word in protest, but ascended the chariot as soon as he was asked to.

Krishna took the chariot to a spot far removed from the noise of the city. He left Satyaki behind and he descended from the chariot holding the hand of Karna. They walked some distance and when they were alone Krishna began to talk to Karna.

Krishna said: "Karna, you are righteous by nature. You are a good man. Why are you bent on helping a sinner like Duryodhana? You know full well that he is in the wrong. You are well-versed in the Vedas and the Vedangas, you have buried yourself in the study of the shastras and you know the nuances of dharma. Why then do you persist in being part of the machinations of Duryodhana? Why do you do it?"

Karna smiled slightly and said: "Krishna, what you say is true. It is not right for a righteous man to associate with a sinner, but my position is different. The affection I have for Duryodhana is so great that I am blind to his faults. He is my dear friend. There was a time when the world turned its face away from me because I am a Sutaputra. I was insulted and ignored because I am a Sutaputra. When I was sorely hurt Duryodhana was the only man who did not pay any attention to the stigma which stained my name. I will recount to you in detail what happened then. I remember it only too well.

"Many years back I had come to Hastina to make a living. The Pandava youths and the sons of the king had just completed their training in archery in the Ayudhashala of Dronacharya. Drona had refused to teach me archery because I was a Sutaputra. It was after this refusal that I went to Bhagavan Bhargava to learn archery from him. But even there my birth dogged me. When he knew that I am a Sutapurtra he was prompt in cursing me.

"Anyway, at the time when I arrived in Hastina, there was going on a tournament which had been arranged by the Acharya to let everyone see the proficiency of his pupils in handling the weapons fit for the sons of kings. I had absolutely no place there, but I was watching the 'prowess' of Arjuna, and I was hearing the praises showered on him: that he was a great archer and there was no one to equal him. I could not brook this. There arose in my mind a desire to put him in his place, to let the people know that there are others who can be as good as he is if not better. I rushed up to the stage and challenged Arjuna. But then the fact that I was a Sutaputra got in the way. I was not allowed to compete with him because he was the son of a king while I could boast only of a charioteer for a father. Again I was insulted and I was very unhappy.

"At that moment, when the entire city of Hastina was laughing at me and my audacity in challenging a son of the Royal House, Duryodhana was the only man who saw me suffering and he took me under his wing. He made me king of Anga and he asked nothing of me except my friendship. Years have passed since then, but I will never forget that magnanimous gesture of Duryodhana. There are only two people in this wide, wide world who love me and who wish me well. One is my mother Radha and the other is my friend Duryodhana. I have never been enamored of this life of mine on this earth. I am indifferent to it. But then, so long as I am alive, my life belongs to these two: my mother and Duryodhana."

For a moment Krishna was silent. He then said: "You are right. It is not always easy to pay the debt of gratitude. I want to ask you something else. Have you any idea as to your birth? Do you know who your mother is?"

Karna shook his head and said: "No, I do not know much. But I guess that she must have been a highborn maiden and that I am the son of a noble house. I assume that she must have been the daughter of some noble king. Her palace must have been situated by the side of a river which caressed the walls of her palace. Evidently she was more concerned about her reputation than her newborn child and so, as soon as I was born, she placed me in a basket and let me float on the river. This is my guess.

"Radha was the woman who rescued me from this basket and she took me to her bosom. She brought me up. My real mother never once thought of me, I am sure. And neither was I interested in trying to trace her. I am not interested, Krishna. But why this talk of something which has been buried in the past? What benefit will result by my knowing about my mother?"

Karna was silent for a while and then spoke again. He said: "Believe me, Krishna, I am not unhappy about this. I have a mother, the sweetest of mothers, and she is everything to me. She is proud of me. My past has been forgotten by everyone. I have forgotten those early days of pain and humiliation. Why should I waste time talking about this?"

Krishna's eyes were full of compassion, and he looked at Karna with soft eyes. His eyes were wet with unshed tears. He spoke in a very gentle voice. He said: "Karna, it is true, what you say. Your mother does belong to a great and noble House. She is a princess. When you were born she was a maiden and since she was afraid of the censure of the world she abandoned you. But you are wrong when you say that she had no thought for you. She has not been able to forget you. Now, at the present moment, she is the mother of more than one son, but her heart is full of sorrow because she remembers you and thinks of the injustice she has done you."

Karna was stunned by the words of Krishna. He could not speak because of the rising excitement in him. He said: "Krishna, this means that I am not a Sutaputra! I am a Kshatriya! Can it be possible? Is it true? From the way you talk it seems to me you know who my mother is. Tell me, is she alive? Will it be possible for me to see her? Tell me everything, Krishna. I am eager and excited. Please put an end to this suspense and tell me the truth."

Krishna took Karna's hands in his and held them firmly. He said: "Karna, compose yourself and prepare your mind to hear the truth. It will be a shock to you, but you will have to bear it."

Krishna could not proceed because of the emotion in his own heart. He had to hurt this good man and he did not relish it. But he had to. He spoke almost in a whisper: "Your mother is alive. She has five sons. They are great heroes who have no equals in this entire world."

Karna felt that he would choke. His breath came in great gasps now. He murmured: "Five sons who are great heroes!

What are you trying to tell me? Do you mean the Pandavas?" His body was trembling because of the emotion in him.

Krishna said: "Yes, Karna, the five Pandavas are your brothers. Your mother is Kunti. You are her firstborn and so you are the eldest Kaunteya. You were born when Kunti was unmarried."

"My father?" stammered Karna. "Who is my father?"

"This divine being whom you worship every day: this god whom you have chosen as your istadaiva, Surya, is your father."

Karna could not bear it. He fell down in a faint.

Krishna was sitting patiently by his side. His hands were stroking Karna and his eyes were raining tears. After a while Karna woke up from his faint and he spoke in anguish. He moaned: "Indeed I am the most unfortunate of all beings. Surya is my father and Kunti is my mother. Yudhishthira, that image of dharma, is my younger brother; the valiant Bhima, the brave Arjuna, the handsome Nakula and the wise Sahadeva are all my brothers. And yet, all these years I have been branded as a Sutaputra. Evidently Bhargava must have seen me with his inner eye and realized that I was a kshatriya."

Tears were flowing from his eyes and so they sat silent. Karna wiped his eyes with his hands and said: "Krishna, you have known this secret of my birth for a long time, evidently. You have kept it from me all these many years. Why did you have to tell me now? I was happy in my ignorance. After being silent till now, you have decided to come to me with the truth. WHY? Why did you tell me now? I was happy in my hatred of the Pandavas. Now, now that I know the truth, my mind has been upset and you have shaken my firmness. I am floundering in unhappiness."

Krishna's heart was ready to melt with pity for this noble man. He said: "Karna, there was a reason behind this act of mine. I wanted to save you from death. You are well-read. You are acquainted with dharma and you are righteous. There is a rule that a son born to a woman when she was maid becomes the son of the man whom she marries later. And so, you are a Pandava and the eldest Pandava, as you were born before Yudhishthira was. You are my cousin as your mother happens to be my father's sister.

"Come with me, Karna. We will go to Yudhishthira. All the five brothers will fall at your feet. You will be the king of this Bharatavarsha. Yudhishthira will be the the Yuvaraja. The Pandavas will be your slaves and they will obey your slightest wish. My dear Karna, you are a hero and you are a righteous man. Your days of pain are at an end. Accept the monarchy of this earth. Make your mother and your brothers happy. Come, come with me now."

Karna was listening to Krishna. His mind was in great turmoil. He said: "Krishna, you are affectionate towards me and you have told me this because of this love you have for me. You tell me that I am a Pandava, that I am the son of Kunti Devi, and my father is Surya. But Krishna, my mother threw me into the river long ago. She did not want me. The one who brought me up, who gave me life and love, is Radha. Athiratha was my foster father. It is not easy for me to think of breaking away from this bond to them. My loyalty is to Duryodhana. I have sworn that I will stand by him to the end, that I will fight a duel to death with Arjuna. How can I forget this solemn oath of mine? You have shown your love for me and you have told me that I will be showered with the affection of the Pandavas. But you cannot tempt me with all these, Krishna. You dangle a kingdom in front of me and ask me to change sides. Do you think I will break my oath and accept all that you offer?

"If I break my oath my reputation will be gone. I know that the Pandavas have you by their side and that they will be the victors in this war. My death is just as certain as their winning the war, but I have the comfort of knowing that by this death my fame will remain in the world of men. I have been unfortunate all through my life. I had but one desire for which I was living: that was a fight with Arjuna in which I had hopes of killing him, or die while fighting. Now you tell me Arjuna is my brother. After knowing this, how can I enjoy the fight with him? But be that as it may, I am determined to fight this duel with Arjuna. By revealing the secret of my birth now, you have broken my spirit, you have killed my enthusiasm. Why did you do it?"

Krishna spoke not a word. Karna caught hold of his right hand and said: "Krishna, promise me that you will keep this secret locked in your heart. No one should know about it. If, by chance, Yudhisthira should come to know of it, he will not accept the kingdom. He is righteous and he should not know that I am his brother. You are the friend of the Pandavas. The Pandavas are all heroes and they have right on their side and they have Krishna who has sworn to protect them. They are sure to come out victorious in the war.

"I know that our side is doomed. But Krishna, even the setting sun can cast a rainbow across the sky and make his exit beautiful. Even so, I will try to die gloriously. My death is certain. And believe me, I am not unhappy at the thought of my death. There is always the possibility that the tears I have shed over my drab and futile life may help to form a rainbow which will illumine my last moments. There can be no rainbow without water-drops, Krishna. Come Krishna, our meeting is at an end. We will meet again on the battlefield."

After a while Karna spoke again. He said: "As I said before, the victory of the Pandavas and the death of Karna are both certain to take place. This war which is imminent is, in reality, a yagna. In this yagna, Bheeshma, Drona and all the Kauravas will be burnt to ashes. I am just waiting for the end of the war. I am sick of this life of mine. I am eager to reach the heavens meant for those who die in war. I will see you again in the heavens perhaps. I will meet my mother, and my brothers, too. I bid you farewell, Krishna. You have achieved your purpose to kill my enthusiasm but, strangely enough, I am not angry with you."

Karna walked away from there and ascended the chariot. In silence the chariot went back to Hastina and they rode towards the house of Vidura.

Karna and Kunti

Krishna went back to Upaplavya. In the meantime Vidura was giving daily reports to Kunti about the goings on in the court. She had heard all about the mission of Krishna and its failure. War was now a certainty and Kunti was worried about the outcome of the war.

Bheeshma, Drona and Karna were great heroes and they were arrayed against her sons in battle. It was not wise to underrate these heroes and their prowess. Kunti was really concerned about the duel which was to be fought between Arjuna and Karna. She knew that Karna was her son. She knew too that he was capable of killing Arjuna. She was drawn towards both of them and she did not want either of them to die. She thought, "Why should I not go to Karna and tell him that he is my son? I will try and win him over to Yudhishthira's side. If I ask a favor of him he will surely grant me that as I am his mother and he is reputed for his generosity. They say that he has never refused anyone anything." Having made up her mind, Kunti decided to go and see Karna the next day.

It was midday. On the banks of the river Ganga, Karna was in the habit of offering worship to Surya. Kunti went alone to the banks of the river and she saw Karna absorbed in the worship of the sun. He stood with his arms upraised and his eyes were closed. He was lost in meditation. Kunti went and stood behind him. The heat from the sun was intense and she shielded herself with Karna's upper cloth and waited for him to complete his worship.

The worship was over and Karna opened his eyes. He saw a woman standing behind him and she was wilting like a lotus. She had covered her face with his upper cloth as she could not bear the heat of the sun. He was surprised at the sight of the woman.

Tenderly he led her to the shade and after saluting her he said: "Devi, I am Karna. It seems to me you belong to some noble family. You are unused to hardships as this sun seems unbearable to you. What can I do for you? I have made it a rule to give away gifts after the worship of the sun. If you have come to me with a request, if it is within my power to grant it to you, I will consider it a privilege."

Karna stood still waiting for her to speak. Years back she had wrapped him up in a piece of silk and placed him in a basket. She had set the child afloat on the river and now, after so many years, she was seeing him. Her mind went back to that day and she remembered asking the gods to protect her child. She had sent her prayers along with the waters which were carrying her child farther and farther away from her. She had said: "My child, Varuna and the god of wind, Vayu, will protect you. That woman will indeed be fortunate who will give you her milk. I envy her." With these words she had sent the child away from her and he now stood before her asking her if he could grant her anything.

Her prayers had been answered and the child had been reared by Radha. She could not take her eyes off him.

Karna stood patiently waiting for her to speak. Finally Kunti said: "I do not know if you have seen me or no, but I have come to you to ask you a favor."

Karna said: "Devi, I do not know who you are. But something inside me clamors that I should know you. It seems to me I have met you before, somewhere, some time. Your figure, your tears, your voice, all these seem to be familiar. I do not know why this should be so as I have never met you before.

He frowned and added: "I am trying to remember where

I have seen you before." Suddenly he shouted: "Ah yes! I have it! You are the woman of my dreams. I am certain you are the same woman."

Kunti smiled faintly and in an amused voice she asked: "Will you explain to me what you mean by your 'dream woman'? I will sit here by your side. I am not in a hurry to go. I have come to spend some time with you. Tell me."

Karna said: "I have not told anyone else about this dream of mine except my mother Radha. But I want to tell you about it. I want to open my heart and talk to you about it. And this is a matter of wonder to me. I wonder if you know about it or not, but my name is Radheya. My mother is Radha. But then, she is not my real mother. My father Athiratha found me floating on the waters of the river Ganga. He gave me to his wife Radha and she has been my mother ever since then and I call myself Radheya. It has always been a matter of great sorrow to me that my mother should have left me to the mercy of the river when I was born. Perhaps this is why I began to dream of her.

"My deep sleep would be disturbed every time by this mother of mine. The dream was the same every time. A woman would appear in my dream. Her form would be draped in silks and brocade and I guessed that she was someone highborn. She was decked in jewels and I would try and see what she was like. But her face would always be covered by the edge of her *Sari* and I could never see her face. Often she would lean over me and keep gazing at me as I lay sleeping. Her tears would fall on me hot and burning. I would wake up and ask her again and again: 'Devi, who are you? Why do you weep?' She would reply in a voice choked with tears: 'I have done you a grave injustice and so I am weeping. I want to have you all for myself. But you have been separated from me for ever and ever. I am heartbroken because of that. I can meet you only in your dreams. Perhaps some day you may come and see me by melting into my dreams. This is why my heart is full of pain and longing.' She would then disappear. I would often ask her: 'Devi, will you not let me see your face once? Just once?' But she would vanish and I could never be able to see her face.

"Time passed slowly and as time passed, my sleep was

not haunted so often by this strange woman. After a while the dreams came to an end. She came to me no more. Possibly she had become a mother again. I thought to myself: 'She must have been my mother. She has forgotten me since she now has other children to fill the emptiness in her heart.'

"Tell me, Devi, who are you? Why have you come to me? How is it possible for you to open this old wound of mine and make it bleed again? Tell me."

Kunti bowed her head down. She did not know what to say. She took some time to harden her heart and talk. She said: "You have guessed right. I am 'the woman of your dreams', as you call her. I am Kunti, the mother of the Pandavas. And . . . and I am your mother, too. You are my first-born."

Karna spoke with emotion: "Kunti, the fortunate mother of five great heroes has come to poor unfortunate Radheya to ask a favor of him! Is this a vision or a waking dream? The woman of my dreams is here in front of me and she is telling me that she is my mother!"

He stared at her for a long minute and she looked at him with her soft, sad eyes. A moment and they were in each other's arms. Tears were drenching them.

Karna said: "Mother, finally you have come. You do not know, you can never guess, how many times I have dreamed of this moment! I have thought of you so often and I have been aching to have your arms around me. I have thought of you, but you have not spent a moment in remembering me and my long life of pain and frustration.

"How often have I tried to raise the veil and look at your face when I dreamed of you! Mother, you gave me birth, but all these many years you have stayed away from me. You have made me so unhappy by staying away from me. After all, I wanted very little. All I wanted was a look at your face. I wanted to see you. Anyway, you have come now and you have accepted that I am your son. Can I ask for any greater happiness than this?"

Kunti turned her pain-filled eyes towards Karna. He was smiling and he said: "Mother, I have known who I am. Till very recently I did not, but I have been told that you are my mother and that my father is this sun whom I have been worshipping. Because of your fear of the censure of the world, you threw me into the river Ganga. I know all these facts."

Kunti was taken aback and she asked: "I had not imagined even for a moment that you would be aware of this secret which has been locked in my heart all these years. How did you know? And, when you knew that I was your mother, why did you tarry? You should have come to me. Why did you wait for me to come to you? Tell me why."

Karna smiled, but his eyes were full of bitter pain. He said: "Mother, yesterday, just yesterday, Krishna came to me and told me everything. But let us forget all that. Mother, come and sit by my side and talk to me. I know that this happiness will not, cannot, last very long. I want to drink the cup to the dregs as it will soon be snatched from my hands. Let me bathe myself in the waves of happiness which envelop me now. Let me be happy because my mother is with me. It is stupid to talk now. I will keep silent and in silence I will remain, tasting this happiness."

Kunti had found her long-lost son and Karna, his mother, for whom he had been aching all these many years.

Karna woke up from this dream of happiness and said: "Mother, you do not know how grateful I am to you for your coming. I do not know how long this will last, this presence of yours. Maybe a few months more or, perhaps, a few hours. But I will have to wake up from this dream. Tell me, mother, why did you come to me now?"

Karna had stood up from her side and his voice was more firm now. The first moment of emotion had passed and he was waiting for her to speak. Kunti said: "Karna, do not call yourself Radheya any more. From now you are Kaunteya. You are my son. I now have six sons and not five. I am very happy today."

Karna's eyes were filled with tears as he said: "Mother, oh my dear mother, tell me why you came to me now. Why have you decided to tell me the story of my past now? You know well that I would have loved to be called Kaunteya. I am proud to know that I am the son of Surya and Kunti. But, mother, I will continue to be Radheya till I die. Mother, you can never know, never realize how unhappy I am. But the wish of the Maker is that I should be unhappy. Forget my pain and my unhappiness. Tell me what it is you wanted of me. You said that you had come to me to ask me a favor."

Kunti was silent for a while; then, wiping her tears, she said: "My child, my son, you have been made to suffer indignities which were countless because the world thought of you as a Sutaputra. The world did not know your parentage. But now the dark days are over. The dreadful shame which was your heritage because of your birth is at an end. You did not know about it, but you are the brother of the Pandavas. Because you did not know, you hated them; but now it is at an end, this hatred of yours. It is not right to hate your brothers. This enmity must end. Come with me. I will take you to your brothers. I know that you will be lord of the world. Your brothers will fall at your feet and worship you. You will attain the peace for which you have been aching all these years. Abandon your friendship with the sinful Kaurava, Duryodhana, and come with me. This was the favor I wanted you to grant me. This is why I have come."

Karna looked at Kunti and said: "Isn't it strange that on two days consecutively two great souls have come to me and offered the monarchy of the world to me? I have been told that I will be lord of the entire Bharatavarsha. Mother, the ways of Fate are indeed strange. I have not even had time to consider these suggestions. Tell me, mother, if I do accept your words and come with you, what will happen?"

"Why, you will be united with your brothers," said Kunti. "Arjuna will be your slave instead of your sworn enemy. With the aid of the Pandavas you will be able to rule this world. Balarama and Krishna will be your well-wishers and they will be by your side. You will no longer be called a Sutaputra but you will be a Pandava."

When she was saying this a strange voice could be heard from the heavens. It was Surya and he said: "My son, Kunti's words are for your well-being. Listen to her."

Karna was looking at his mother. He spoke not a word and his eyes were full of pain and anguish. He broke the silence finally and said: "Mother, you may not be aware of it, but I have been very angry with you. This anger was all aimed at the mother who was wont to haunt my dreams. This anger is not aimed at you, mother. It is because of that dream-mother that I had to bear insult after insult all these years. My name, my recognition in the world of heroes, my very life were all ruined because of her. Thousands of doubts would rise in my mind, but I paid no heed to them and I tried to ignore the pain which had filled my life.

"Looking at you today, at your soft, sad eyes, that anger is gone. It has vanished like snow upon the desert's dusty face. I am dying to be petted and loved by you. Radha, my mother is dear to me, very dear to me, but even the love I have for her seems to grow less when I look at you. My heart is eager to become one with my brothers and the very thought thrills me. My heart cannot hold so much happiness."

He rushed to her and held her in a close embrace. Surya was pleased to see this meeting between mother and son.

After a while she spoke and said: "My son, come, we will go together and you can meet your brothers."

Karna's heart was ready to break because of his sorrow. He spoke in a voice harsh with pain. "Mother, that will not be possible. I cannot come with you."

"Why?" asked Kunti in amazement. "Why is it not possible? Why do you hesitate? I assure you that you will be welcome there."

Karna said: "Mother, under no circumstances will I betray my friend Duryodhana. I am bound to him in many ways. I owe him a great debt of gratitude. Mother, you remember only too well that you abandoned me the moment I was born. I have been a Sutaputra all these years. No one would accept me as I was lowborn. During those difficult days it was Duryodhana who took me to his heart. Drona had refused my request. I had gone to Hastina where a tournament was being held, but when I challenged Arjuna, I was ridiculed by everyone because of my birth. Mother, you were there, surely! You must have recognized me then. But you did not lift a finger to help me out of my predicament. I do not wish to remind you of the old days and make you unhappy, but I want you to know what happened then. When everyone was laughing at me, when Bhima taunted me with cruel words, Duryodhana was the only man who welcomed me into his heart. It will be unrighteous on my part if I abandon him now.

"Mother, there is a storm in my heart. Till today I had no one to love me except Duryodhana, my friend. But today you have come to me with your heart full of a mother's love. I am assured of the devotion of my brothers. My heart is ready to break at the thought of all this. I am so full of love for each and every one of you. I could do anything for the sake of this love which has been offered to me. BUT, I am not prepared to give up Duryodhana. I owe him so much and you will never understand the bond between us. I am a slave to affection and he has given me affection. He has grappled me to him with hoops of steel and it is not possible to free myself from this bond of love. I cannot forget my love and my duty because of this newfound love which you offer me. You have come and you have made me happy for a few moments, but I will have to forget this entire episode as I cannot be false to my friend. My mind and my body belong to my friend. I offered them to Duryodhana long ago, on the day of the tournament.

"Mother, my end is very near. I have, by my own efforts, won a name and some fame for myself. I do not want to lose this little acquisition of mine. I know that everyone who is siding with Duryodhana is destined to die on the field of battle. I am not excluded. We will soon be dead. As for the Pandavas, not a hair of their heads will be touched. Krishna has taken it upon himself to protect them. You need have no worry about them, mother.

"As for me, I was born with divine armor and earrings which promised me immunity from death. But then Indra took them away from me to save his son, I know. It has been my rule in life never to refuse anyone anything and Indra's begging bowl was not empty when he went away. You asked me to grant you a favor. It is my misfortune that I cannot grant you that. But then, I cannot send you back empty-handed either. I swear, mother, I swear that I will not fight your sons EXCEPT ARJUNA. I will not fight with my other brothers. I will certainly fight with Arjuna, but I know the end: he will kill me. But what does it matter? You will still have five sons. They have always been the five Kaunteyas and so it will be till the end. Do not worry. I will die and you will still be the mother of five sons. Death will come to me and not to Arjuna. You will always have five sons. If, by chance, Arjuna should die, then I will be there to make up the number five. But that is an improbability. Karna is destined to die. You should go home now, mother; it is late. Let your mind be at peace as your sons will be safe. Leave Karna to his fate and go in peace."

Kunti was beside herself with grief. She was trembling. She had found her son and lost him, too. Her heart which had been empty all these years was even more desolate. Like a streak of lightning which illumines the sky for a moment and leaves it darker than before, even so this brief interlude served to make her more unhappy than she had been before.

Karna could see that she was suffering. He clasped her once again in his arms and said: "Mother, it is not possible to alter what has been etched in the Scrolls of Fate. Your tears and my prayers will not alter the future. What has been destined to happen will happen. Do not try to stem the tide of Fate. It is ineffectual. It is but the work of Fate: your birth and mine, and the events in our lives. Bless me. Grant that I will soon reach the heavens which may hold for me all that I have been denied on the earth. Wash my pain with your tears, mother. I feel that your tears are more precious to me than the waters of a coronation bath. Your tears are more sacred than the waters of the river Ganga. Mother, go now; a dream of a different kind is in store for me and for you, too."

Kunti had become weak, so weak that she could not stand up. Pain and sorrow had drained her of all strength. Karna raised her up with love. Again and again mother and son embraced each other.

Finally Karna released her from his embrace, and slowly she began to walk away from there. Kunti saw him stand away from her and she had to go. Slowly, very slowly she walked away from there. Karna stood rooted to the ground and looked at her until she disappeared from his sight. When he could see her no more he stood there still, looking into empty space. The gods in the heavens saw this sight and they mourned the fate of this noble man.

The Begging Bowl of Indra

It may not be out of place here to relate the incident Karna mentions to Kunti, his losing his kavacha and kundalas.

Karna was the son of Surya and Arjuna's father was Indra. Naturally, Surya was partial to Karna and so was Indra to his son Arjuna. Both these gods were worried about the welfare of their sons. Even before the great war was fought, Indra began to worry about Arjuna. He knew about the valor of Karna. He also knew that the kavacha and the kundalas, which had been the gifts of Surya to his son, had given him immunity from danger of any kind. Weapons could not hurt him and he was invincible. There was every possibility of Arjuna proving to be the loser in an encounter between the two.

Karna was asleep on his snowy bed and he dreamed that a noble-looking Brahmin stood by his side. He spoke to him: "Radheya, you worship the sun every day. You have made it a rule that you will not refuse anything to anyone who comes to you after this midday worship. Indra knows about this. He is the father of Arjuna and his sympathies are, naturally, with him. He will come to you and ask you to give him your kavacha and kundalas. You know that it will spell danger to you if you part with these. Give anything to Indra but not these. This is a matter of life and death for you. I have come to warn you about this impending disaster so that you may act wisely. Save yourself at any cost."

Karna said: "My lord, you seem to be extremely concerned about me and my welfare. You are my well-wisher. I can see that. Please let me know who you are. I want to know who can be so fond of me as to warn me with so much concern."

The Brahmin told him that he was Surya. Karna was thrilled that Surya, his Ishtadaiva, had come to him in his dream and he said: "My lord, I am infinitely grateful to you for warning me about the coming of Indra. But you know that I can never refuse anyone who asks for anything immediately after my worship of you. Ever since I adopted this rule I have been exceedingly happy and I have found a semblance of peace because of this vrata. I am happy while giving gifts to others. If I have been asked to part with something which is dear to me, the thrill of giving it away is greater than usual. Even if I am asked to give my life, I will not say 'No'. It is not possible for me to refuse anyone anything.

"If Indra comes to me and asks me for something which will be of help to the Pandavas, I will not be able to refuse him that. Even if I know that it is harmful to me I will have to give it. This is unavoidable.

"My lord, I have never been fond of this life of mine. I am eager for only one thing and that is a good name. And so, my lord, it will not be possible for me to refuse a gift to Indra when he asks me for it. I am not prepared to lose the good name I have earned for the sake of saving this life of mine. Maybe I may live forever if I say 'No' to Indra, but then I will not be able to live with myself after that. What is the use of life if the infamy one has earned lives after his death? I will be talked about in disparaging terms by men in aftertimes and the very thought of it makes me shudder. I prefer death to the infamy I will be courting if I agree to your suggestion.

"I know, too, that the Pandavas will win the war which is sure to be fought. The Fates have already decided that the Kauravas will be destroyed completely. I know that my death is inevitable. Why then should I break my vrata and lose my good name?

"I assure you, to me fame is more dear than my life. Fame

is the very life breath of good men. Infamy is death and who will welcome infamy willingly?

"In this body which is so transient, life tarries for a while. And to protect this bundle of bones and flesh if one should incur disgrace it is indeed foolish. Fame purifies one's life. For the sake of earning this fame I am prepared to die. My lord, I am grateful to you for your concern. All the same, I cannot refuse Indra his request. Please grant that I fight well."

Surya said: "Child, you are very dear to me and to protect you I came here. I wanted to warn you of the danger which is threatening you. Think of the others and not of yourself. Think of your queen and your sons who love you so much. If you die no doubt your fame will live in the minds of men, but how will it help those who depend on you? Your dearest wish has been to defeat Arjuna in battle. If you lose your kavacha and kundalas you will not be able to realize the desire which has been in your mind all these years. While they adorn your body, not Brahma, nor Narayana, nor any of the gods can touch you. It is foolish to lose such a precious possession for the sake of an ideal."

Karna was on the point of tears. He said: "Your affection makes me speechless. It is overpowering, but, forgive me my lord, I am unable to accept your advice. You are my god and yet I am unable to obey you because this rule of mine cannot be broken. My life is worthless when compared to the sanctity of my vrata."

Surya said: "Child, I am immensely pleased with you for your firmness. I am proud of you." After blessing him, Surya disappeared and Karna went back to sleep.

The next day, when the sun was at the zenith, Karna completed his worship. Indra donned the guise of a Brahmin and came to Karna. Seeing him, Karna asked: "Bhagavan, how can I serve you? You have come at a time when I am in the habit of giving away gifts. If you have come to me with some wish in your heart, please let me know."

The Brahmin said: "Radheya, I do not want anything else. All I ask is the gift of your kavacha and kundalas."

Karna said: "Your desire is strange. These have been part of me even since I was born. It is not easy to sever them from my body. Ask something else of me: some astra or gold and silver which will be more useful to you. Why do you want these?"

The Brahmin said: "I want nothing else. If it is true that you are generous enough to give anyone anything one asks, then give me these. I want only these from you."

Karna looked at him for a moment. He then laughed and said: "My lord, perhaps the glitter of these has charmed you! I can assure you, they are but ordinary. Their power is great but they are priceless only for me. They have been dipped in the nectar of the gods and they have been grafted on to my body. They are meant to protect me from danger and death. They are precious only to me and will be of no use to you.

"And there is this to be said: I have given my word to my friend Duryodhana that I would fight with Arjuna and kill him. These two are very necessary for me if I should keep my word to my master and friend. Please do not ask me to part with them."

The Brahmin was adamant. Karna laughed with great amusement and said: "My lord, I know who you are. You are Indra, the king of the heavens. You have been famed to be the greatest of givers. The world is drenched with water and Mother Earth owes her greenery to you and your bounty. Such a great donor now stands before me asking me for a gift. It is really most embarrassing to me. You know, my lord, that disaster will follow my parting with them. Still, be assured that I will not say 'No' to you. Please take what you have come for."

A divine light was seen on the face of Karna as he sat down and cut off his armor and kundalas from his body. He laid them at the feet of Indra. They were drenched with the blood of the noblest of all the kshatriyas and Indra stood still as Karna said: "My lord, take them. I have laid them at your feet."

Karna was happy because he had made the supreme sacrifice for the sake of his honor. Tears of happiness were in his eyes. Indra was overcome with emotion. His eyes were wet and flowers rained on Karna as he stood there with his palms folded.

Indra said: "Karna, yours is a noble soul. You are great. Surya had warned you about my coming. But you would not swerve from the path of dharma which you have been following all these years. I am extremely pleased with you. Ask any boon of me. I will grant you anything you desire."

Radheya said: "Indra, to make a gift and to take something in return does not become a man. The grace of giving will be gone if such a thing were to happen. And yet, I will ask of you a boon. Do you know why? Men in aftertimes will consider this act of yours as heinous and they will talk ill of you. Your reputation will be tainted because of this. I want to spare you this infamy. This is the reason why I will ask you to grant me a boon. If I accept something from you in return for what I have given you, then there will be no talk of this act of yours or about the unfairness of it.

"People will then say: 'No doubt Indra did him an injustice but Karna accepted something in return for the favor he granted.' You will escape the censure of the wise by granting me a boon. So I am going to ask you for it. Give me the Shakti with which you destroyed your enemies."

Indra was astonished by the words of Karna, but was also immensely pleased with him. He said: "Karna, today you have conquered the lord of the gods. I will grant you what you have asked for. First let me grant you something which you did not ask. Your body which has been hurt because of the removal of the kavacha and kundalas will be rid of the wounds and scars which mar the body. You will be as handsome as you were before. I will grant you the Shakti you have asked for. You will be able to use it just once. You will certainly kill the one whom you wish to kill. Once this happens, this Shakti will come back to me. You cannot use it a second time."

Karna was happy. He said: "I will not need to use it twice. I have but one enemy and it is enough if I have the Shakti to use it on him once, just once."

Indra said: "I know what is in your mind. You wish to kill Arjuna. But Radheya, so long as Krishna is there to protect him, nothing will harm Arjuna."

Radheya said: "Indra, I have every hope of winning this war. Though I have lost my armor and my kundalas I have not lost hope. I am eager to fight and I hope to win."

Indra replied: "Radheya, your winning and losing are immaterial as far as the war is concerned. You have today won for yourself a great name and greater fame by this gift of yours to me. From today men will call you KARNA and that will be because of your generosity. Your name will live for ever. You said that I am a great giver because my rain clouds empty themselves on the earth at my behest. The idiom is: 'Like Parjanya in giving'. But from today the world will say: 'Like Karna in giving'. Accept my blessings. I have to go."

Indra turned away from him and again there was a rain of flowers on Karna.

This story of Karna proves to us the greatness of his character. Karna was noble. He was righteous and he was ever firm about keeping his promises. He was endowed with the qualities which have made Sri Rama such a great figure in the epics. At the cost of one's life, one's promise must be kept. This was the rule which governed the House of the Ikshvakus and Rama was famed for it. The generosity, fearlessness, greatness, adherence to promise were characteristics of Rama, and Karna had the same qualities. Because of his loyalty to a sinner the nobility of this man was concealed like the glorious sun behind a cloud. But Vyasa has so narrated the story of the heroes that we have been allowed to get flashes of the real nature of this man again and again.

Rama's nature has been reflected in that of Karna completely. Krishna said: "Karna, you are a righteous man." Kunti said the same thing. Vyasa has only proved the truth of these statements by the narration of this incident in detail.

Among the characters in the Mahabharata that of Karna is unparalleled. His valor, his nobility, his generous nature and his truthfulness are famed throughout the world. He was like a glittering star which had been concealed behind the dark cloud Duryodhana, and could not shed its entire brilliance on the world. Vyasa has taken particular trouble to lift the dark cloud again and again and he has allowed the greatness of Karna to reach the heart of every human being who reads the Mahabharata.

Karna makes his appearance once again at the end of the epic. The war is over. Yudhishthira and his brothers have gone to the banks of the Ganga to offer the final ablutions to those who were dead. Pindas had been offered to the Pitris and water. This was done to satisfy the departed souls.

Kunti went to Yudhishthira. She stood silent for a moment and then said: "Yudhishthira, you have forgotten to make the offerings on behalf of one more departed soul."

Krishna heard her and he knew what was in her mind. But he said nothing.

Yudhishthira asked her: "Mother, who could I have forgotten?"

"Karna," said Kunti.

Yudhishthirs was surprised and slightly irritated by her words. He said: "Karna? What do you mean, mother? Karna was a Sutaputra and he was our enemy. What makes you think that I should be the one to perform his final rites?"

Kunti said: "Child, Karna was not a Sutaputra. He was a Kshatriya."

"Kshatriya?" asked Yudhishthira. "Whose son was he?"

"He was my son," said Kunti in a firm voice. "Yudhishthira, Karna was your elder brother."

"Mother! What are you saying?" asked Yudhishthira.

Kunti replied: "It is the truth. Karna was my son." She then told Yudhishthira the entire tragic story of Karna.

Yudhishthira's heart was broken. Arjuna and he with the others were ready to kill themselves when they knew about Karna. Krishna had to comfort them and talk them back to sanity.

The story of Karna is one of the most tragic and noble stories in the Mahabharata. He was a great soul and Vyasa has done full justice to this character by bringing to light all his many noble qualities. There are some exemplary men in the Mahabharata and Karna is one of them.

Yudhishthira

War had become unavoidable. In the holy spot of Kurukshetra were assembled the armies of the Kauravas and the Pandavas. A strange event occurred which is worth relating.

Yudhishthira removed the armor he was wearing and placed it on the top of his chariot. He placed all his weapons too by its side. He descended from his chariot and walked with bare feet towards the place where Bheeshma was stationed. Bhima, Arjuna and the twins, along with Krishna, spoke nothing but walked with him. They knew not what he was planning to do, but they went with him. All eyes were on Yudhishthira and they could not make out why he was doing it. What was he trying to do? Bhima and Arjuna tried to ask him, but he spoke not a word. Krishna knew what the reason was.

Yudhisthira was walking towards the chariot of Bheeshma. The army parted and gave way. When he reached the presence of his grandfather, Yudhishthira fell at his feet and took the dust on his head. He then said: "Grandfather, please grant me leave to begin the war and bless me and mine so that we should be victorious in this war."

Bheeshma said: "Child, Krishna is there by your side. Why then do you have any doubt about winning the war? You will win. I have to fight for Duryodhana as I owe this debt to him and his father. I am helpless."

After this Yudhisthira came back to his camp. He put on his armor and he took up his weapons. He blew the conch called Anantavijaya and the war was on.

In the Middle of the Night

When Arjuna began to fight, the affection he had for his grandfather was so strong that he could not fight properly. Krishna did not approve of the halfhearted manner in which Arjuna was fighting. Krishna said: "Arjuna, what are you trying to do? It will not be possible to win this war unless your grandfather is killed. Fight with more concentration. Do not let your emotions get the better of you." But Arjuna persisted in his weak and unwilling fight.

Krishna was furious. He said: "If you are not willing to put your heart into the fighting, I will fight and finish this old man. He has got to die or else you must be prepared to lose the war." Krishna jumped out of the chariot. He had his chakra in his hand and he ran towards Bheeshma.

Bheeshma was delighted. He said: "My lord, can anything be more glorious than this? To die at the hands of Krishna is indeed an honor to be desired."

Arjuna was dumbfounded by the suddenness of Krishna's action. He fell at his feet and said: "Forgive me, Krishna. Under no circumstance should you break your oath that you would not touch a weapon during this war. I will do what you ask me to."

He promised to fight with Bheeshma and bring about his end. This is another instance when Krishna, for the sake of the Pandavas, was prepared even to break his word and take up a weapon.

Arjuna had promised that he would put his heart and soul into the fighting and now the enemy camp saw a different Arjuna. He was destroying the army of the Kauravas ruthlessly. But he could do nothing about stopping the old man and his fury. He was like a forest fire and he was burning up the army of the Pandavas. The Pandavas were now certain that the hope of victory would remain but a dream unless Bheeshma died.

In the night Yudhishthira was sitting desolate in his tent. They had assembled to discuss the day's events and he said: "Krishna, my heart is full of despair when I think of our grandfather. He is so powerful and he is fighting like a young man. I have no hopes of winning this war."

Krishna tried to pacify him with the words: "Do not lose heart so easily, Yudhishthira. There must be some way out of this. I am wanting the death of Bheeshma. You are all dear to me and Arjuna is my particular friend. I am prepared to cut myself into little pieces if it will help Arjuna in any way. Arjuna has sworn that he will kill Bheeshma and I do not want his oath to become false. If only Arjuna would fight with real fury he can kill the old man, but he has so much respect for his grandfather that he loses interest in fighting when he is placed before Bheeshma. All of you are suffering from the same weakness: you allow your affection and emotion to gain the upper hand. This is the reason why you are unable to kill Bheeshma and proceed victoriously.

"I am the only one capable of this task because I am beyond the sway of the opposites. Happiness and sorrow, pleasure and pain, good and bad, are all equal as far as I am concerned. I do not see any difference between a tiger and a deer as I am far beyond the reach of emotions. To me there is only one thing important and that is to do one's duty properly. Nothing else interests me. If Arjuna cannot kill Bheeshma, I will have to do it for him as it is essential that Bheeshma should die, and the sooner the better."

Yudhishthira's eyes were full of tears. He said: "What you say is true, Krishna, but I will not let you break your oath for the sake of the Pandavas who are not doing their duty properly. I will not be the cause for this. I can think of only one way out of this. I will go to my grandfather, fall at his feet and ask him how we should set about killing him."

After an initial surge of disbelief, they saw that it was the best thing to be done under the circumstances. All six of them went to the tent of Bheeshma in the middle of the night when the army on either side was sleeping.

There was silence in the tent of Bheeshma. They entered all together and fell at his feet. Bheeshma was greatly excited at the coming of these youngsters and said: "Krishna, looking at you and these children, I am extremely pleased. I am very happy to see you." He spoke to each one of them and blessed them all. He then said: "Arjuna, I was extremely pleased and proud when I saw you on the field. Your skill and dexterity with the bow is unparalleled. I am greatly impressed by your prowess, but tell me, why have you come to me now, in this time of the night when the whole world is sleeping? What brought you here to the enemy camp?"

Yudhishthira spoke in a distressed voice: "My lord, you had told me that victory would be mine. But then, as long as you are there on the battlefield we cannot hope to win." He paused for a moment and wiping his tears he said: "You know how we hate to think of your death. But we have to find some way to kill you or else there is no hope for us. We have nothing but love, respect and veneration for you, but still we have to kill you. You will have to tell us how this can be achieved. How can we bring about your end?" Yudhishtira was sobbing and so were the others.

Bheeshma said: "My dear child, you are speaking only the truth. It will be impossible for you to win as long as I am alive, and I do not want to live. I am not fond of this life of mine and I want to die soon. But it is not easy to kill me. I am pining for death, but the boon which has been granted to me by my father prevents death from approaching me. I am happy that you asked me how you should kill me. I will tell you.

"Only two people can bring about my end. One is Krishna and the other is Arjuna. If one of these will grant me my freedom from this bondage I will be happy."

Arjuna heard the words of his grandfather and he began to cry. Bheeshma said: "Child, listen carefully. So long as I am engaged in fighting I am invincible. If, however, I throw down my weapons, then it will become easy enough to kill me. There is a way to make me do this, too. I will never fight with a woman. Even if it is a man who was a woman in his previous birth, I will not fight with him. Even if his name has something feminine about it, I will not fight with him. This has been my rule.

"Remembering this, if you manage to bring Shikhandi before me I will throw away my weapons. Shikhandi was a woman in his previous birth. Amba, the daughter of the king of Kasi, is born again as Shikhandi. If Shikhandi should appear before me asking for a fight I will refuse and throw away my bow. Arjuna, you should remain behind this Shikhandi. The moment I throw away my bow you should shoot your arrows at me. Remember my instructions. My blessings will always be with you. Go, my children, and win the war. I will also find peace after death which will come to me soon now."

Bheeshma's face was glowing with the anticipation of the peace which had been denied him all these years. Krishna smiled very sweetly at him and said: "Grandfather, give up your life and be happy after that."

Arjuna heard all that his grandfather had been saying and said: "Krishna, this is wrong. This is a dishonorable thing to do. How can I bring myself to do what will be the most unchivalrous act which a Kshatriya can think of?"

Krishna said: "This is the dharma of Kshatriyas and you will have to observe it. Consider it to be your dharma, your duty, and without any hesitation do what you have been asked to do."

Arjuna accepted his words unwillingly and they all left the tent of Bheeshma. Every heart was full of sorrow except that of Bheeshma. He was ecstatically happy because freedom was near at hand for him at last, at long last.

The Deaths of Bheeshma and Abhimanyu

It was the tenth day of the great war. Bheeshma was very happy. He was certain that death would come before sunset. Arjuna, naturally enough, was listless. He was thinking of the moment when he would have to kill his old grandfather. He told Krishna: "Krishna, I have been watching all these days. Every time Shikhandi came in front of him grandfather would turn his chariot away from there. I see the reason for it only today. I will remember what he told me last night. I will see that Shikhandi is with me and I will not lose sight of him. We should protect Shikhandi from the army of the Kauravas."

The army was arranged in the asura vyuha by Bheeshma and Dhrishtadyumna had taken resort to deva vyuha for his army. The fighting began with great enthusiasm on either side. The arrows of Bheeshma were like live coals and they were burning up the army of Yudhishthira. Duryodhana was very pleased with the course of events when he saw the fury of Bheeshma and the helpless manner in which the army of his enemies was struggling against his onslaught. He looked at the face of his grandfather and was amazed at the look of ecstasy on it.

Shikhandi, in the meantime, had approached Bheeshma. Bheeshma spoke with contempt and said: "Shikhandi, you are not a man and to me you will always be a woman. I refuse to fight with you."

Shikhandi said: "Bheeshma, you may say what you please. But I will not go without fighting with you." He began to send arrows aimed at Bheeshma, who would not respond to his challenge. The Kauravas were puzzled by the lack of response from their leader and the Pandavas hastened to protect Shikhandi.

Duryodhana rushed to the side of his grandfather and said: "What are you doing, Pithamaha? If you do not fight back we will be destroyed by the Pandavas."

The old veteran said: "Duryodhana, my child, right at the beginning of the war I told you that I would be the sole destroyer of the army of the Pandavas. Again and again I will repeat to you that the Pandavas will come out of the war unscathed. Arjuna will kill me and I will not be able to harm Arjuna. The gods themselves will not be able to harm the Pandavas as Krishna is there to protect them. I will die today and I will clear the debt I owe you. This is what is making me happy. Believe me when I tell you that I am waiting to die."

Drona told his son Ashwatthama: "My son, I am seeing evil omens. I fear that some dreadful calamity is to visit us."

Bheeshma was getting sick of the entire fighting. The sun was wheeling his path towards the west and the impatience of the old man was growing. He said: "Yudhishthira, please make haste. Release me from this old and sere body."

The Pandavas brought Shikhandi to the fore and Arjuna was stationed right behind him. Bheeshma would not fight back when Shikhandi's arrows hit him. He flung his bow down and he sat still, refusing to fight. His mind was busy with memories of his earlier achievements and he told himself: "I am still able to defeat all of them, but enough injustice has been meted out to these unfortunate sons of Pandu. I wish them well and I would like them to win this war. The purpose of my life has been attained. I have to abandon this body."

He heard voices from the heavens and they said: "This decision of yours is laudable and it is good for the world."

Shikhandi continued to send his arrows at Bheeshma but the old warrior refused to fight back. His bow had been abandoned and Krishna saw this. He said: "Arjuna, this is the moment when you should rush in. Shoot your arrows at Bheeshma who is without his bow."

With pain in his heart Arjuna did what he was asked to do. Hundreds of arrows pierced the hardened frame of Bheeshma.

Bheeshma fell. There was panic in the army of the Kauravas. When he fell, he asked to be placed on a bed of arrows. Arjuna prepared it for him and lying on it Bheeshma said: "I have fallen. But I will hold my life till the coming of Uttarayana. When the sun's chariot turns towards the north I will abandon this earthly frame and be one with the gods." Duryodhana fell down in a faint. He had not thought that this would happen. The army was standing still and everyone stood around the fallen hero.

Bheeshma said: "My head is not comfortably placed. I need a pillow." Poor Duryodhana rushed to him with a pillow and the old man smiled sadly at him and said: "Duryodhana, my child, this is not the pillow for one lying on the battlefield." He turned towards Arjuna and said: "Arjuna, you should provide me with the proper pillow."

Arjuna shot three arrows into the ground and they held the head of the dying warrior in place.

Duryodhana sent for physicians to alleviate the pain of his grandfather but the old man would have none of it. He called Duryodhana to his side. He caressed him with his old and gnarled fingers and said: "Child, this Krishna and his friend Arjuna are the sages Nara and Narayana. Now that I am gone, there is absolutely no chance of your winning this war. Make peace with the Pandavas. Let me be the one to have achieved it by giving up my life."

Duryodhana heard him, but his words had no effect on him.

Bheeshma closed his eyes. As he lay on his bed of arrows, he forgot all about this world and the pains therein. He was lost in the contemplation of the Lord and so they left him.

Bheeshma had been granted the boon that he could die when he pleased. This was the gift from his father. He waited for the coming of Uttarayana, but as far as the world was concerned he was gone. The world had lost a truly heroic soul.

The gods were raining flowers on the fallen hero, and the Pandavas as well as the Kauravas stood around him with tears streaming from their eyes. But he was immune to it. It was the end of the first act in the tragic drama.

Duryodhana was heartbroken when Bheeshma fell, but the war had to go on. After along consultation with the others he came to the decision that the great army of the Kauravas would now be led by Dronacharya, their Guru. Everyone approved of his choice and Drona was appointed commander of the army. Drona spoke words of encouragement to Duryodhana and told him that he would try his best to destroy the Pandavas.

Drona was a past master in the art of fighting and he was a genius in the formation of the different vyuhas. He arranged the army as a padma vyuha. This was considered to be impenetrable. There were only two great heroes in the Pandava army who could break up this vyuha and they were Krishna and Arjuna. The third was Pradyumna, the son of Krishna, but he was not fighting.

On the day Drona arranged this vyuha, Arjuna was engaged in a fight which was taking place far away from the field of battle. Since Arjuna was away, there was no one who could penetrate into the vyuha and the Pandavas were helpless.

Drona was stationed at the entrance of the vyuha and his army was bent on the destruction of the army of the Pandavas. Yudhishthira was at a loss as to what should be done at this juncture.

Abhimanu, the son of Arjuna, came to his uncle and said: "I know how to break this vyuha and enter it. But I do not know how to get out of it. I have not learned that."

The army of the Pandavas, in the meantime, was being mowed down by their Acharya. Finally Yudhishthira and the others said: "Let Abhimanyu break into the vyuha. We will all be with him. We will follow him and when the vyuha is broken there will be no need to worry as we will be there to destroy the entire formation. We will protect our child and no harm will come to him."

Yudhishthira said: "Abhimanyu, child, your father is far away from here and he is engaged in fighting with others.

This Acharya of ours has arranged this army as a Padma vyuha as you know and he is causing havoc in our ranks. I did not want to risk sending you into the vyuha, but there seems to be no other course open to me. Break into the vyuha, my child. All the heroes on our side will be with you and they will follow you. You will just have to lead the way. They will protect you. There will be no need to come back from the vyuha as you would all have destroyed it together."

Abhimanyu was a hero, a maharathika, and he was proud to have been asked by his uncle to take upon himself the great responsibility of saving his army. Everything depended on him and his prowess as his father was far away in another part of the field. He was certain that he could break the vyuha.

Abhimanyu entered the field and with him were the others: Bhima, Dhrishtadyumna and Satyaki along with Nakula and Sahadeva. To the chagrin of Drona, Abhimanyu broke into the vyuha in a matter of moments and the Pandava host was now advancing with the speed of wind.

Jayadratha was the brother-in-law of the king. He now came to the rescue of the Kauravas. He came between Abhimanyu and the others who were there to protect him. He blocked the entrance to the vyuha through which the youngster had passed and the Pandava heroes could not go inside. They could do nothing about it.

The tragic story of the young hero, Abhimanyu, is only too well-known: how he was trapped inside the vyuha, how he fought like a lion and how seven maharathikas surrounded him and, together, killed him.

When Arjuna returned to his camp in the evening he was told about the great tragedy, about how the Kauravas had managed to trap his son in their vyuha and how Jayadratha had played the major role in the slaughter of his son.

Arjuna's wrath was fearful and he took an oath. He said: "I swear that I will kill Jayadratha before the sun sets tomorrow. Let the entire army of the Kauravas guard him, let the gods from the heavens come down to aid him. It will not be possible to stop me from killing him. I swear on this sacred Gandiva of mine that I will do this. If I happen to fail in this, I will fall into a blazing fire and be turned to ashes."

This impulsive oath of Arjuna was frightening and there was a deadly silence in the Pandava camp. They did not want to think of the morning. If Jayadratha could not be killed then everything would be lost. Abhimanyu was gone and now Arjuna was doomed unless he accomplished what he had sworn to do. If Jayadratha were too well-protected by the Kauravas? If he refused to be exposed and if the sun should set before Arjuna could encounter him in a duel? Thoughts like these were chasing each other in the minds of all of them and a feeling of fear was prevalent. But Arjuna was sure of himself. He plucked the string of his Gandiva and the noise filled the four quarters of the earth and there was a semblance of hope in their hearts.

No one slept that night in the camp of the Pandavas. Nor did the Kauravas find any peace. They had committed an atrocity which was unparalleled in the history of Bharata, but they were not sorry about it. They had been celebrating their victory. They heard the twang of the Gandiva and that surprised them. They were under the impression that, after the killing of Abhimanyu, Arjuna would lose heart and would turn his face away from the field of battle. Before they could try and make out the reason for the twang of the Gandiva, they heard the notes from Krishna's Panchajanya, and the conch seemed to sound the death knell for all their hopes. They waited for their spies to come and tell them what was happening. Very soon they came and they brought with them the news of Arjuna's oath and his decision to kill Jayadratha.

Jayadratha was shivering with fear. He said: "There is only one way in which I can save my life. I will run away from here. Arjuna is a righteous fighter and he will never kill one who has run away from the battlefield."

Duryodhana and the others said: "Do not be afraid. We are all here and Acharya Drona is here to guard you. We are not women; we can fight too. We will guard you. And think of the great good fortune in store for us! Once the sun sets, Arjuna will kill himself and after that the war is as good as ended. The Pandavas can do nothing without their beloved Arjuna, and he is sure to die tomorrow."

Krishna was greatly worried. It was up to him to see that Arjuna's oath was fulfilled. It was as though the killing of

Jayadratha was now his responsibility. He told Arjuna: "My dear Arjuna, you were too impulsive in taking that oath. You should have thought about it first and you should have talked it over with me. But it has been done and there is no use in talking about it now. We cannot retract your oath."

Arjuna said: "Krishna, how can I face Subhadra? You should go to her and help her bear this sorrow. I cannot."

Subhadra was lying in a faint and it seemed as though she were dead. She woke up when Krishna went to her. She said: "How could it happen, Krishna? When you were around, when his famed father was still alive, how could my child have died? How could you let it happen to him?"

Krishna said: "Subhadra, Abhimanyu was a great warrior. He was killed in a treacherous manner. It was a heinous crime. We will avenge his death. Do not weep, my sister."

Krishna could not sleep that night. The bed which was covered with snowy silks would not grant him any rest: he tossed about, and thoughts were crowding into his mind as he considered the possibilities of Arjuna's killing Jayadratha. Nature herself seemed against it. It was Dakshinayana and the sun would set very early and so the time granted them was less than it would have been at other times. The killing should be quick. Jayadratha should not be allowed to escape death. If he was, Krishna would lose his friend and that meant he would have to break his own oath that he would establish Yudhishthira on the Kaurava throne.

In the middle of the night Krishna summoned Daruka and told him: "Daruka a crisis is facing us. You have heard of the oath of Arjuna. As for me, I have sworn that I will not touch a weapon during the fight except the whip with which I drive the horses of Arjuna. But then, I cannot live without Arjuna. If, for the sake of the killing of Jayadratha, I have to take up arms, I will do so. Perhaps Drona and Karna will have to be killed before we can approach Jayadratha. I will not hesitate to use my chakra and my mace Kaumodaki if necessary. And so, Daruka, please keep my chariot equipped with all my weapons and you should be in readiness. Remember to let my banner fly in the chariot, the banner of Garuda. Yoke my horses to the chariot and cover them with armor. If I should call to you, come at once with the ratha."

Daruka said: "My lord, you have commanded me and I will keep everything in readiness as desired by you. But you have taken Arjuna under your wing and that means no evil will befall him. I am sure of it. Go to sleep, my lord. Everything will turn out to be auspicious and Arjuna will come back to the camp victorious."

Drona and Jayadratha

It was the fourteenth day of the great war on the field of Kurukshetra. All the many heroes were thinking of just one question: would Arjuna be able to kill Jayadratha before the sunset? Yudhishthira was extremely depressed and he told Krishna: "You are my sole support and anchor. I depend on you to steer us through this dreadful predicament. Arjuna has taken this reckless oath and his life is in your hands."

Arjuna entered the tent of Yudhishthira and fell at his feet asking him for his blessings. His face was calm and there was a look of determination which was pleasing to all. As for the war which was fought on that day, *records* have it that it was one of the most eventful days of the great war.

The Kauravas were, of course, bent on protecting Jayadratha. Arjuna was like the fire at the end of Time and he was burning up the army. His wrath was something not human.

In the midst of the fighting Krishna said: "Arjuna, I am afraid the horses are too tired to proceed any more unless they are rested for a while. They are thirsty and we have to reach the spot where Jayadratha is hidden. It is quite some distance from here and we cannot achieve our purpose if the horses fail us at the crucial moment." Arjuna jumped out of the chariot and began to fight on foot.

Krishna said: "Arjuna, I need water. Where do I go for

it?" Vyasa here describes the skill with which Arjuna shot an arrow into the ground and made water collect there and form a tiny lake out of which the horses drank their fill.

The fight between Satyaki and Bhoorishravas was also fought on this day. The situation was tense. Satyaki and his enemy were engaged in a dread combat. At one stage Satyaki was unconscious, and while he was senseless Bhoorishravas tried to kill him. Arjuna had to intervene and cut off his right hand. This was against the code of dharma as no one is allowed to interfere when a duel is being fought, but Satyaki was Arjuna's favorite pupil and he had to be saved at any cost.

Bhoorishravas turned his face away from the fight and he decided to give up his life by performing what was known as Prayopavesha. He spread kusa grass on the ground and sat on it adopting the Padmasana. He set his mind on the Lord and turned his thoughts away from the world. It was at this moment that Satyaki rushed up to him and with his sword cut off the head of Bhoorishravas. No one approved of this action of Satyaki. Bhoorishravas had turned his face away from fighting, and to kill him then was unjust.

Arjuna did not approve of it either, but the gods in the heavens approved of it. It had been destined that the death of Bhoorishravas would be at the hands of Satyaki, and so it had to happen thus. The argument was strange, but then the ways of the gods are strange too, and no one can dispute what has been ordained by them. And so the event was a closed chapter as far as the war was concerned.

The real purpose of the war that day was the killing of Jayadratha. The sun was relentlessly hastening towards the west. There was not time enough for the chariot of Arjuna to reach the spot where Jayadratha had been hidden. He was protected by no less than seven Maharathikas. Arjuna's chariot was not allowed to proceed at all. The entire army was engaged in stalling Arjuna and in crowding around the intended victim, Jayadratha.

Finally Arjuna managed to reach Jayadratha. They fought a duel. Arjuna was sending his sharp arrows at him but Jayadratha was a fighter of no mean order. He was a Maharathika and there was no sign of his tiring. The sun's rays were losing their heat indicating that soon the sun would set. The sky had begun to turn red. If Jayadratha could hold out till sunset then everything would be all right, thought the Kauravas. Arjuna would have to kill himself as he had sworn. The death of Arjuna would mean that the war was at an end.

Krishna realized the seriousness of the situation. He said: "Arjuna, it will be impossible to kill Jayadratha before sunset. Time is conspiring against us. I know what is going to happen. I will have to do something about this. Listen to me. The moment I say: "Now, shoot," you should use the most powerful astra at your command and aim it at Jayadratha. Leave the rest to me. I will have to use my Maya in this case. You have to obey me implicitly and that is the only way open to you."

Krishna summoned the chakra mentally and he commanded it to cover up the disc of the sun. The moment this happened darkness descended on the field like a curtain. The Kauravas were jubilant while Arjuna was dejected beyond words. There was shouting and dancing among the Kauravas and Jayadratha was unbelievably happy. Darkness had fallen, the sun had set and with a heart full of joy Jayadratha raised his eyes to the sky and smiled in triumph.

Krishna said: "Now, shoot and see that the head of this sinner does not fall on the ground. Make the astra carry it to his father's lap."

Arjuna had the Pasupata ready in his hand and he sent it towards Jayadratha. It cut off his head. The chakra moved away from the disc of the sun and they could see him in all his glory.

The Kauravas saw all that was happening. They could not save Jayadratha and they saw his head traveling in the air. His father was engaged in offering the evening prayers to the sun. When he had completed the worship the head of his son fell on his lap. When he stood up trying to see what it was, the head broke into a thousand pieces.

It is worthwhile discussing this event. Krishna was prepared to break his oath for the sake of the Pandavas. He deceived the Kauravas by hiding the sun with his chakra. Krishna's sole purpose was to see that Jayadratha was killed

—by right means if possible, but if that failed, by deceit.

It is true that everything was not quite straightforward in this context. But the end justified the means. Jayadratha had to be killed because he was wicked. He had been part of the unjust killing of Abhimanyu and he had to be punished. Krishna's purpose was to lessen the burden of mother earth and this he was accomplishing with swiftness and cleverness.

The Kaurava army was sunk in depression after the death of Jayadratha. Duryodhana began to labor under the impression that in his partiality towards the Pandavas, Drona was not fighting properly. His heart was not in the war, thought Duryodhana. He accused Drona of this and added: "If you do not put your heart and soul into the fighting, then the prospect of winning this war seems distant. We will lose." Drona was nettled, but he spoke words of comfort to the Kaurava and promised to do his level best to destroy the entire Pandava host.

"Massacre" is the word that comes to the mind when one thinks of the five days when Drona led the army of the Kauravas. Ruthlessness was apparent in every incident and the Brahmin who had chosen to be a Kshatriya was behaving like a heartless butcher.

There was a rule in the wars of those days that a divine astra should not be used unless there was great provocation. It was also the rule that an astra could be used only against a recognized warrior who was conversant with the use of astras. But Dronacharya began to use the astras against the entire army made up of ordinary soldiers who knew nothing of these astras. At one fell blow an army made up of twenty thousand men was destroyed. This was cruel.

Krishna told Yudhishthira: "Yudhishthira, this Acharya of yours is well-nigh a rakshasa and not a brahmin. He is fighting an unfair and unjust fight. It is not possible to defeat him. If he continues to destroy our army as he is doing now, soon there will not be even one man left in our army. We will have to think up some way of killing this man. Things should be so engineered that Drona willingly turns his face away from the thoughts of fighting. I can see only one possibility. If he should be told by you that his son Ashvatthama is dead, then he will lose heart and give up fighting. Nothing else will influence him."

Yudhishthira was not pleased at the thought of speaking a lie for the sake of winning the war. But Krishna convinced him that he had to do so for the sake of the innocent men in the army who were being massacred ruthlessly by this one man, the commander of the Kaurava army.

There was an elephant named Ashvatthama in the army of the Pandavas and Bhima promptly killed it. He then went to his guru and said: "Gurujee, Ashvatthama is dead." When he heard these words Drona fell down in a faint. Waking up he pursued the fighting. He now took up the Brahmastra in his hand and invoked the mantra for it.

The rishis and gods had assembled in the skies to watch the great fight. And they spoke to him: "Dronacharya, why do you persist in this Adharma? Death is better than this ruthless behavior of yours. Look towards us and throw away your weapons. You are well-versed in the Vedas and the Vedangas. A brahmin like you should not resort to cruelty."

Drona heard the voice from from the heavens and his enthusiasm waned. He looked around him and he saw Yudhishthira in front of him. He asked him: "Child, tell me, is Ashvatthama alive or is he really dead?"

Drona was sure that Yudhishthira would never utter a lie. Yudhishthira was incapable of speaking. Krishna hurried to his side and said: "Remember what I told you. If this man continues to fight as he has been doing till now, the field will be empty as far as our army is concerned. He is pursuing an unrighteous path and it is your duty to save the men by speaking this untruth. It is a sin to speak lies I know, but when the situation is desperate and when nothing else will serve the purpose an untruth is allowed.

Yuidhishthira was convinced that he should now tell a lie to Drona. So he said: "Ashvatthama is dead," and softly added, "Ashvatthama, the elephant."

It has been said that the chariot of Yudhishthira had always been inches above the ground, but when he spoke this lie it touched the ground.

Drona was lost to Duryodhana. Bheeshma had gone, and now Drona. There was a pall of despair in the Kaurava army.

Duryodhana had to admit now that the Pandavas were well-nigh impossible to defeat. But Krishna was pursuing his task relentlessly. The burden was getting lighter on the earth, but it had to be lightened still further.

The Death of Karna

The gates of the temple of death were wide open and Krishna was sending the heroes to their death one by one. Bheeshma was gone, Jayadratha had followed him; and now Dronacharya. The Kauravas did not know what they should do now. After Drona's death the king conferred with his counselors and decided to make Karna the commander of the army.

When they had assembled to discuss the future course of action, Ashvatthama said: "The next commander should be a powerful warrior, he should be quick in action and capable. With such a commander at the helm of our army success is sure to be yours. Duryodhana, there is no dearth of warriors in your army. There is no need for you to be so desperate. We are all ready to lay down our lives for your sake. I feel that, at this juncture, the only person to infuse courage and hope into the minds of our people is Karna. Bheeshma and Drona fought for you and died. But then there was, in their hearts, a lurking affection for the Pandavas and this made them soft at times. Their hearts were not in the fight.

"But Karna is different. He will fight with all his heart. I suggest that you make Karna the commander of the army."

Duryodhana was pleased with the suggestion. He approached his friend and said: "Radheya, all my hopes are centered in you. I have laid the entire burden on your shoulders and it is up to you to lead us to victory."

Karna was excited and pleased with the words of the king. He said: "My friend Duryodhana, I am happy to know that you have so much confidence in me. Tomorrow I will kill Arjuna and place the world at your feet."

On the sixteenth day of the war Karna entered the field of battle as the commander of the army. Yudhishthira saw the vyuha which had been arranged by Karna and said: "Arjuna, see what a difference these sixteen days have made to all of us. This army of the Kauravas was immense on the first day when our grandfather led it. And it has become so small now. If you kill Karna we can then be sure that victory is ours."

No one could withstand the fury of Karna and the sharpness of his arrows. There was an equal response from the Pandava army and soon the field was covered with the dead forms of men. The first day was a day of slaughter on either side. Both of them had lost a large portion of their army. The king was unhappy as Arjuna was still alive.

Late in the night Karna went to the tent of Duryodhana. He knew that the king had been disappointed in him. Duryodhana was alone. Radheye went to him and said: "My friend, I am unhappy that I could not keep my promise to you: that I would kill Arjuna today. But tomorrow I will certainly achieve what I have been aching to all these years. Listen to me.

"I am superior to Arjuna in every way. I am more skillful and I am the better archer. My famed bow is bigger and stronger than his Gandiva. I desire nothing else but the death of Arjuna tomorrow. But, Duryodhana, there is one factor where Arjuna is superior to me. He has as his charioteer Krishna who is extremely capable in steering the horses on the field of battle. There is no one to equal him: no one except Salya, the lord of Madra desa. If he can be coaxed to hold the reins of my horses then victory is within my reach."

Duryodhana promised him that he would try and ask Salya to be the charioteer for Karna.

Karna went back to his tent. Try as he might, he could not sleep. He knew for certain that this was his last night on the earth. He knew that victory would be the share of the Pandavas because Krishna's protecting hand was there.

Even if Salya agreed to be his charioteer, how could he face Krishna? Radheya spent the entire night in speculations like this. Suddenly he thought of his two mothers. He and Radha were bound by a very strong love. But Kunti's soft sad eyes seemed to be looking at him. He could not forget her and the few hours he had spent with her on that one day.

Karna was a great archer and he was an adept in the art of war. But he had been cursed by his guru that he would forget all that he had learned when he needed them most. Another curse further weakened him. His chariot would sink to the ground while fighting, and that would be the moment when he would meet his death. Karna knew all this only too well.

But Radheya was not concerned about these factors. He had lost all interest in life. To him death meant a sleep, a long, long sleep from which he need never wake up. He wanted to be free of the debt he owed his friend and death was the only way he could attain it. Once he was dead, he would not have to insult the Pandavas again and again by taunting them, by helping Duryodhana in his sinful acts against them.

He knew that Krishna was full of compassion for him. He too loved Krishna very much. The only possible way out of his predicament was death. He was eager to welcome death which would release him. The night passed thus for him.

The next day Duryodhana went to Salya and laid his problem before him. Salya was, of course, beside himself with anger. He thought it was an insult to be asked to be the charioteer to a Sutaputra. He said: "I am an anointed king and he is a Sutaputra. You ask me to do this. How dare you insult me and my birth?"

Duryodhana pacified him and told him how his entire life was in his hands. He entreated him and said: "You are far superior to Krishna, and Karna is, of course, much more powerful than Arjuna. This is the only chance I have of seeing the defeat of the Pandavas. Victory is very near and it is up to you to help me achieve it."

Salya had to agree to his suggestion and Duryodhana heaved a sigh of relief. Everything would be perfect from now on.

Salya brought the chariot to the tent of Radheya. After making a pradakshina to it, Radheya ascended the chariot. He prayed to his father Surya and he then spoke to the king: "My friend, I will fight till the breath leaves my body. I will see you after the sun sets and I will bring you news of my victory. This is what I hope, but it is all in the hands of Fate."

This was to be their last meeting. Radheya knew it and tears blinded him as he took leave of Duryodhana.

Salya laid the whip on the flanks of the horses. Evil omens were seen. Radheya knew full well what these omens meant. As he was driving the chariot, Salya spoke nothing else but words praising the prowess of the Pandavas.

Karna said: "Salya, your words are perfectly suited to your name. They are like arrows and they hurt abominably. But I am not bothered by them now. In the vast expanse of the Lord's creation man is an insignificant nothing. Bheeshma is gone, Dronacharya is gone. I know that I cannot avert the death which is sure to claim me. My only desire is to leave a good name behind. Men in aftertimes will remember me as a good and righteous man. I am bent on doing my duty. I will fight to the best of my ability and I will reach the heavens meant for those who die on the battlefield."

Karna first encountered Yudhishthira. He broke his chariot and broke his bow too. Yudhishthira's body was hurt by the arrows of Karna. Soon he was weaponless and he looked at Karna. The noble warrior said: "Yudhishthira, you should never have been born a Kshatriya as you are a brahmin by temperament. I will not kill you. I desire only to fight with Arjuna and kill him."

Yudhishthira was so hurt that he had to go to his tent and rest a while. He was in great pain. He was sorely hurt too by the words of Radheya. He was peace loving by nature and he had never been happy at the thought of this war. Every day only served to prove to him how futile the war was. But the war had begun and he could not turn away from it.

He was impatient for the war to end. But that was possible only when they won a victory. He was also displeased with Arjuna because he had not killed Karna yet. And Radheya saying that he was better fitted to be a brahmin was hurting him.

Arjuna heard that Yudhishthira had been hurt by Radheya while he was in his tent. He was concerned about his brother and so rushed to see him. Krishna and Arjuna found him alone in the tent and they could see that he was greatly depressed. His face was a study in pain and anger too.

Yudhishthira looked at them both and thought that they were coming to him with the news that Karna was dead. He said: "Arjuna, you have today made me very happy. I was hurt by Radheya. His arrows and his words were both sharp. I can see that you have killed him and have come to tell me about it."

Arjuna said: "My lord, I am unhappy because I have not killed him yet. I have not been able to meet him in single combat."

Yudhishthira was disappointed at the words of Arjuna. He became angry and said: "Arjuna, throw away this Gandiva then. I will enter the field and accost this Radheya." Arjuna lost his temper too. Krishna had to pacify them both. Arjuna swore to his brother that he would come back to him only when he could do so with the news that Radheya had been killed.

When they had come out Krishna said: "Arjuna, your impulsive oaths are proving to be very hard for me. I have to see to it that you keep your word and it is not easy. Radheya is a hero and a warrior of no mean order. He has defeated so many kings single-handed. I do not consider him to be your equal because he is superior to you in many ways. He is glorious like fire, quick like the wind, and in anger he is like Indra. That is Radheya. He is brave and he is righteous. He is famed for his generous nature and he has won a great name for himself. The one fault in him is his association with a sinner, Duryodhana. He is on the side of Adharma and that is the only shortcoming of Radheya."

Arjuna said: "I am glad you told me all this but I have you by my side and with your blessings I will be able to win in the end. Take me to where he is and place my chariot there."

Radheya saw Arjuna coming towards him and he told Salya: "My lord, I will fight my best now and win the world for my master and friend. I have sworn that I will kill Arjuna. If, however, I should die in this encounter, what will you do?"

Salya was full of admiration for Radheya and with his heart full of emotion he said: "Radheya, if you become a victim of Fate, I will kill Krishna and Arjuna and avenge your death."

Salya's words put new life into Radheya and he was excited at the duel ahead of him. The duel for which he had been waiting so many years was to be fought now and he was ready for it.

Krishna was encouraging Arjuna with the words: "Arjuna, you will certainly win this war. You cannot lose. But if, by any chance you should die, you can rest assured that I will kill Salya and Radheya. My anger will burn up the entire universe. But do not worry. The sun may lose his heat and break up into a thousand pieces, but you will not lose in this fight with Radheya."

Ashvatthama saw the chariot of Arjuna approaching that of Radheya. His mind went back to the previous day when Bhima had killed Dusshasana. Bhima had sworn that he would drink the blood of Dusshasana. And he had done it too and no one could do anything about it. They stood stunned and horrified when Bhima cupped his hands and drank the blood.

Duryodhana had been extremely depressed. Ashvatthama went to him and said: "Duryodhana, look! The two heroes are about to begin their duel to death. My heart is full of sadness at the thought. It is indeed unfortunate that things have come to this. Even now it is not too late. Duryodhana, stop this war which is like the end of the world. The Pandavas are good men and they did not want this war at all. Krishna came to you with an entreaty for peace which you refused. If you say the word the war will stop and even the Pandavas will be happy and so will Krishna. Bheeshma is gone and my father has died. Now Radheya is to die. Stop this war or else the Pandavas will win and not one of us will be left alive."

Duryodhana drew a long breath and said: "You are right, Ashvatthama, you are right. But my brother Dusshasana has been killed. What is the use of my living after that? Let me die fighting. I cannot think of any other path open to me."

The duel had begun and the two heroes bent on killing

each other were stationed face to face. They began with the exchange of arrows and after a quiet beginning the pace altered and soon they were beginning to think of using astras.

Arjuna used the astra presided over by Agni and Radheya replied with Varunastra. Karna now despatched the astra called Bhargava. The army was suffering because of this and Bhima went to Arjuna in a fit of temper and said: "You are fighting like a woman. I may fight better than you."

Krishna said: "Arjuna, remember you are an avatara of Nara. You have been born for a special purpose and do not forget it. Fulfill it. Bring to mind your prowess and fight."

Arjuna took resort to the astra of Brahma. The army was affected but nothing else happened. Radheya sent arrow after arrow at Arjuna and each was sharper than the other. Both were good archers and this fight was more like a display of their prowess than a real fight.

Radheya was feeling that he had dallied long enough with Arjuna. He took up the dread Nagastra. He had decided to use the Shakti given to him by Indra, but unfortunately he had had to use it up the previous day when Ghatokacha was working havoc in their ranks. Indra's Shakti had gone back to him.

Radheya took aim at the head of Arjuna and Salya said: "Karna, not his head. Aim it at his chest."

Karna said: "It is not befitting that a hero should alter his aim. Once is enough for me." He sent the Nagastra at Arjuna.

Krishna saw the dread astra coming towards Arjuna. With a quickness which was like lightning Krishna made his horses kneel down. The chariot was lowered and the Nagastra went just over the head of Arjuna, struck his jeweled crown and passed without harming him.

Radheya was heartbroken. He had no other powerful weapon with him. He tried to summon some of the divine astras, but because of the curse of Bhargava not one of them would come to his mind. His memory failed him and Radheya knew what a helpless puppet he was in the hands of fate.

The protectors of Radheya's wheels were frightened away from there by Arjuna's arrows. After a while one of the wheels of the chariot was caught in the mud. There was no one to guard his wheels and Radheya found himself helpless. His memory had gone and now this added mishap. He descended from the chariot and tried to lift the chariot from the rut into which it seemed to have fallen. And all the time Arjuna's arrows were raining on him.

Radheya looked at Arjuna and said: "Arjuna, this is not right. It is unrighteous to shoot at me when I am engaged in the task of lifting up the chariot. Wait for a while. Let me get up and then we can resume the fighting."

Krishna laughed at him and said: "Radheya, it is ages since you had anything to do with dharma! And you dare to talk of it now! You were there when the Pandavas were sent to the house made of lac. Where was your dharma then? Draupadi was dragged to the court and where had your dharma gone while you sat there watching her? A week, hardly a week has gone by when a child of sixteen was killed by seven maharathikas of whom you were one. Was that dharma? Do not make me sick with your talk on dharma. You have no right to mention that word."

Radheya knew that every word he spoke was true and he spoke not a word in reply. He raised the chariot from the rut and began to fight and again the wheel got embedded in the mud. He had to try once more to lift it up. He had put both arms under the wheels and his muscles stood out like whipcords as he strained at it.

Krishna said: "Arjuna, do not tarry. Before Radheya rises up you must kill him. If he resumes fighting we cannot guess what will happen."

Radheya was on the ground, helpless. He had lost the power to use his astras and his chariot had proved useless. Arjuna's arrows were wounding him all over and finally his head fell on the ground severed by Arjuna's arrow. Karna was dead and the Kaurava army fled from there in panic.

Duryodhana's grief was immense when Radheya died. He was beside himself and he rushed to his grandfather for comfort. The great man was lying on his bed of arrows and to him went Duryodhana, weeping like a child would to its mother when it has been hurt.

Bheeshma said: "What is the use of tears, my child? Your friend died as a Kshatriya should, fighting on the battlefield. There is nothing here to weep about."

Duryodhana asked him: "What are you saying, grandfather? You call him a Kshatriya. Radheya was a Sutaputra."

Bheeshma said: "No, he was not a Sutaputra. He was the son of a Kshatriya woman and he is a Kshatriya."

"Tell me," asked the Kaurava. "Tell me who he was."

The old man replied: "I had no right to talk about it as long as he was alive as I had promised Radheya that I would keep his secret. If you promise that you will keep it to yourself, I will tell you."

Duryodhana's voice was weak with pain. He said: "I swear, I swear that I will tell no one about it."

Bheeshma was silent for a while. He then said: "You will be amazed at the truth when you hear it. Harden your heart so that it can bear the news. Radheya was not really Radheya, child, he was Kaunteya. He was the eldest of the Pandavas."

Duryodhana could not bear to hear the news. He fell down in a faint. When he woke up he said: "I have been the cause of the death of such a noble hero! For my sake he fought with his own brothers and died. He never even hinted that such was the situation. I have killed the greatest of men."

After hearing the words of comfort from his grandfather Duryodhana went back to his tent.

Hope rises eternal in the human breast and Duryodhana would not give up hope. All his warriors had died one after another. With a desire to win, Duryodhana made Salya the commander and he lost him too in a single day.

Eighteen days: only eighteen days were enough to wipe the entire Kshatriya clan off the face of the earth. Krishna had succeeded in lessening the burden of the earth in this short span of time.

Duryodhana

The war was over but Duryodhana was still alive. The Pandavas could not claim victory completely so long as he still lived. The eleven askhowhinis of the Kauravas had been wiped out completely. Not one was alive. Only the king was left. Apart from Duryodhana there were three more who were not killed: Kripacharya, Ashvatthama and Kritavarma. Nothing else was left of that army which was like a sea when the war began. As for the army of the Pandavas, two hundred chariots remained and a hundred elephants, a thousand horses and a few soldiers. The family feud was almost at an end after causing so much havoc, but something more had still to be achieved for the completion of the war and that was the death of Duryodhana.

Duryodhana cast a look of pain on the expanse of the battlefield. There was nothing there except heaps of bodies. Vidura had told him again and again: "You will be the ruin of the entire race of Kshatriyas," and Duryodhana remembered his words. He heard the words as though they were spoken now.

With his heart full of pain and frustration, he went away from there. He wanted to go somewhere far, far away from the scene of devastation that was spread out before his eyes. His limbs were burning as though they were on fire and his eyes lighted on a lake. He told himself that he would enter the lake and find some peace for a while.

While he stood there he saw Sanjaya. The charioteer of the king was miserable to see his prince in this state. Tears sprang to his eyes and Duryodhana gave way to the grief which was choking him.

Duryodhana had lost interest in life and with a forlorn look on his face he was standing on the banks of the lake. Sanjaya came near him. Duryodhana was so unhappy he would not even talk to Sanjaya. There was a listlessness in his gestures which revealed the despair in his heart.

Sanjaya said: "My lord, I am Sanjaya, your father's slave."

Duryodhana composed himself and said: "I am surprised and happy to know that you have managed to escape the fury of the Pandavas. You are alive."

Sanjaya said: "My king, I was in your tent. The Pandavas came there in search of you. Satyaki wanted to kill me, but Dhrishtadyumna stopped him with the words: 'What do we gain by killing him?' Satyaki was still standing with his sword raised aloft when Vyasa came and stopped him. He said: 'Leave him alone. Let him go to Dhritharashtra.'

"I am alive, but, my lord, what has come over you? It seems to me that your mind is all confused and you seem to be lost to the world around you."

Duryodhana said: "Sanjaya, you are right. My mind is all gone to pieces. I am suffering because of my extreme grief and agony. There is no one left to mourn my death. Sanjaya, go to my father because he is the only one who will weep for me and so will you. Tell my father that his son is resting in the depths of this lake: that his limbs are burning and he is in great need of this rest in the waters. I know that I have not long to live. Ask my father to forgive me. Tell my mother that I am unworthy to be the son of a wise woman like her. Tell her, 'Duryodhana has never in his life bent his head before anyone. He now places his head at the feet of his mother in all humility and love.' Ask her to pray for me. Ask her to pray that in my next birth I should be the son of a mother like Gandhari."

Tears were running down his face while he spoke and he took leave of Sanjaya and entered the lake.

Sanjaya was going towards the palace of the king when

he met Ashvatthama, Kritavarma and Kripa. He told them what had happened. Ashvatthama was extremely grieved and said: "Evidently Duryodhana does not know that three of us are still alive. We can fight the Pandavas and there is still hope for our king. He should not lose heart."

The Pandavas were moving heaven and earth to find the whereabouts of the king. They knew that Duryodhana was not a coward and that he had not gone away from them to save himself. They sent men in all directions to find out where the king was.

Evening was drawing near. Kripa and the other two went to the banks of the lake. They called out to Duryodhana and said: "Lord, why should you give in to sorrow and despair? We are still alive: Kripa, Kritavarma and Ashvatthama. We are capable of fighting with the Pandavas and we can destroy all of them. Please come out and let us go to the field."

Duryodhana heard their voices and he was glad. He said: "I am thrilled to know that you, all three of you, are alive. I did not know it till now. It is late in the evening and I am very tired. I will come out early in the morning and tomorrow we will go and fight with those cousins of mine."

Some hunters had come to that lake for a drink of water. They heard these words by chance. They rushed to the Pandavas and told them that Duryodhana had entered the lake and was resting his limbs.

Bhima was wild with joy. Yudhishthira and the others took the rest of the army with them and went towards the lake named Dvaipayana where Duryodhana was "hiding" according to them. Satyaki, the sons of Drupada and, of course, Krishna were with them. Soon they reached the banks of the lake.

The evening was melting into night. Ashvatthama and the other two saw the Pandavas approaching the lake and said in a hurried whisper: "My lord, the Pandavas are coming towards us. We will go some distance away from here."

They went to an Ashvattha tree which was nearby and seated themselves under the shade. They were busy discussing the plans for fighting next morning. They were unhappy because they had to face the fact that the Pandavas had been victorious. They wondered if it would be possible to fight the

Pandavas: they did not know what Duryodhana was thinking of doing. Each one was busy trying to convince the other that all was not lost yet and that they might salvage something out of the destruction which was only too evident.

Yudhishthira went to the edge of the lake. And he said: "Krishna, Duryodhana has hidden himself here inside this lake. But I am not going to let him live. I have got to see him dead."

Yudhishthira then spoke in a loud voice so that Duryodhana could hear him.He said: "My dear cousin, you have been the death of all those who were yours: your entire family and friends. And now you have hidden yourself inside this lake. This is most unbecoming for a hero. Come out and fight with us. Where is your pride and where is your arrogance? Have you no selfrespect? You seem to be a coward from the way you behave; this is the only conclusion we can draw. You are a Kshatriya and you are hailed as one of the heroes of our land. But this act of yours belies all these epithets. Do not cheat yourself of a place in heaven. Are you still fond of this life of yours? After the death of all your kinsmen? Sakuni is gone and Karna is dead. You have always been proud of yourself. Everyone knows only too well about you and your pride. Why do you hide in the water now? Come out and fight. If you manage to defeat us, why, the world will be yours. If you happen to die, you will inherit heaven. Do not be a coward, Duryodhana. Come out and let us see how brave and valiant you are."

Duryodhana heard these taunts from Yudhishthira and he was furous. And he shouted out: "Yudhishthira, stop your inane talk. I did not run away from the field nor am I a coward. I was unhappy because all those who were dear to me are dead. My horse became lame and I had to leave it to die. I saw this lake and I thought of resting my sore limbs here for a while. I am not afraid. Nor am I eager to prolong this life of mine. You must also be tired. Let me rest tonight and tomorrow I will fight with all of you."

But Yudhishthira was firm. He said: "Please do not worry about us. Your concern for our 'tiredness' is touching, but it is unnecessary. We need no rest and so I ask you once again: 'Come out and fight.'"

Duryodhana said: "Yudhishthira, I assure you, I am not fond of life any more, nor is there any desire left in me for the kingdom. All those who were mine are dead and nothing attracts me any more on this earth. Still I will fight with you and prove to you that I am more powerful than all of you. Bheeshma is vanquished and Drona is dead. My beloved Karna is gone. There is nothing left for me on this land which we have fought for. It is now barren and I am prepared to make a gift of the world to you and go away to the forest dressed in ochre robes and deerskin. This land shorn of all that is beautiful is now yours and you are welcome to it, Yudhishthira."

Yudhishthira did not like these words of Duryodhana. He was very angry and he said: "I think you are absolutely without shame: you dare to tell me that you make a gift of this earth to me! I am a Kshatriya. I do not need your charity. I do not have to accept alms from my enemy. I will defeat you in fair fight and take the world from you as my right. There was a time when you were the lord of the world. You usurped the land which was mine and threw us out. When we came back and asked for the land which was rightfully ours you would not give it back to us. Where was this generous nature hiding all these years? Now you are so magnanimous in giving this entire earth to me!

"Surely you have not forgotten the many attempts we made to avert this war! We knew what the consequences would be, but you were blind. Krishna came to you as my Duta and you sent word to me that you would not give me even so much land as can be covered by the tip of a needle. And now, suddenly, you have decided to make a gift of this entire earth to me. You must have taken leave of your senses. The great Duryodhana who was not willing to give me even five villages is now ready to renounce his entire kingdom! What a situation!

"Duryodhana, who said that you have a kingdom which you can give away so generously? Let us forget all this. Come out of the lake and fight with us. For the sake of destroying us you have hatched a hundred plots all these days. And now you want to escape death by cowardice. We are the victors and we want to see you die. Come out. If you meet your death on the field of battle you will surely reach heaven. I am giving you a chance to win a place for yourself there. Come and fight."

Never before had Duryodhana been subjected to so many insults. This proud monarch who had never once heard a harsh word from anyone was now hurt by the words spoken by Yudhishthira. The proud king had never imagined that the soft-spoken, gentle Yudhishthira could be capable of so much anger. He wrung his hands. He wanted one night of rest to relax in the waters but he had to deny himself even this comfort. Yudhishthira's sharp words had hurt him abominably and he could not bear the pain and humiliation.

He said:"Yudhishtira,your righteousness is but a pretense. All of you want to combine and fight with me when I am alone. I have no chariot and there is no army left. I am wounded, too. And yet you have come in a group and I am asked to fight with you. I am not afraid of you. I am only sorry that heroes like you should combine to attack a single man and make sure that he is killed.

"Nothing accompanies a man when he dies except his punya. While under the sway of anger if a man forgets dharma then he cannot be called a dharmatma. You are trying to abandon all thoughts of dharma in this challenge of yours. It is of no great account. You will suffer for this. I am not afraid. I am a Kshatriya. I have been born in the noblest of Houses. I am prepared to fight with all of you. I welcome death. All those who have reached heaven before me will be my companions once again. I am eager to meet Radheya and that is making me eager to die. How can you know the greatness of Radheya? He was a noble soul who made the earth richer because of the years he lived on it. If you do not succeed in killing me now, I will myself engineer my death. I am so eager to meet Radheya. Nothing else matters to me. I am coming out."

Like the sun rising out of the bank of clouds which had been hiding him, Duryodhana emerged out of the lake. He was so handsome, it was unbelievable. His entire frame was glowing and his powerful arms were tensed and ready for fight.

Yudhishthira was pleased to see that he had come out.

He said: "Duryodhana, I knew that you are no coward. You are my dear brother. You will not let the honor of our House be tainted. You are a brave man and a hero. You have today proved to the world that you are a worthy son of the House of the Kurus.

"My dear Duryodhana, you are a Kshatriya and you behave like a Kshatriya. Alone you are prepared to fight all of us and this only shows what a great hero you are. But we are not addicted to Adharma. We do not mean to fight with you all together. You can choose one of us to fight with you. You are also welcome to choose whichever weapon you please. If you happen to win then the world is yours. If you die, you will inherit the heavens. Come, make up your mind."

The Gadayuddha

Yudhishthira could never be angry with anyone for long. When Duryodhana came out of the lake to fight, he was so happy that he made this impulsive offer: that Duryodhana could fight with anyone he chose and with any weapon which he preferred. Krishna was quite displeased with Yudhishthira. But then Yudhishthira was the last man to take back what he had promised and Krishna was worried.

But Duryodhana was a real Kshatriya and he was very touched by the noble gesture of Yudhishthira. He said: "My dear Yudhishthira, it seems as though at the end of my life we are becoming friends! I accept your offer with great pleasure. You are telling me that I can choose any weapon and choose my opponent too! You know well that the only weapon which I have used and which is dear to me is the mace. This Gada has been my companion always and to the end I will place my faith in it. I am ready to fight with all of you or I can fight with you one after another and kill every one of you. Come. I am ready."

Yudhishthira was suffering from the euphoria caused by the friendliness in Duryodhana. He said: "Come, fight with me so that I will have the pleasure of despatching you to heaven."

Duryodhana roared like a lion and said: "I will fight with the one whom you place before me."

Krishna thought he had to intervene. He said: "Yudhishthira, are you aware of your foolishness? You are not capable of killing Duryodhana. There is only one who can face him in Gadayuddha and that is Bhima. Even he is slightly inferior to Duryodhana in skill and power. If this king should accept your offer and if there is a fight between you, then all that we have been fighting for these days will be wasted.

Bhima said: "Krishna, do not worry. I will fight with Duryodhana and I know for certain that his death will be at my hands." Krishna was pleased that Bhima was to fight with Duryodhana.

Bhima called Duryodhana to fight with him. He said: "Duryodhana, the fight has to be between you and me. Try and go back in your memory and remember the many incidents which have taken place. Remember Varanavata; remember the game of dice; remember the insult to our queen in your court. You might have forgotten all of them but we have not. It is not easy to forget. The time of reckoning is here. Prepare yourself to die. I am going to kill you."

Bhima's words were steeped in anger and they were harsh. Duryodhana was his old self. He laughed at Bhima. He looked with contempt at him and said: "Bhima, you are stupid. Your words are meaningless. Do not think that your brave talk will frighten me. Let me see what you can do. For years I have waited for this moment. Indra himself cannot stand before me in this Gadayuddha. Among the Pandavas you are best fitted to fight with me. Come, let us fight."

Yudhishthira said: "Duryodhana, wear your armor. Tie up your locks and if you need anything more, ask for it."

Duryodhana was extremely touched and pleased with the nobility of Yudhishthira. His eyes were wet. Quietly he took up his golden armor and placed his crown on his head. The sun's crimson rays fell on him and Duryodhana looked like the sun poised on the western hills just before setting.

The fight was about to begin. Balarama happened to arrive then. Narada had told him that the Gadayuddha was to be fought between Bhima and Duryodhana. Balarama's pet pupil had been Duryodhana and so the king was extremely happy to see his guru. He felt that this was a good omen.

Balarama said: "I am just coming back from the Tirthayatra which I had undertaken. I heard about this fight. I came to watch you. I have a suggestion to make. The spot called Samantapanchaka is very near. Such a holy spot is this Samantapanchaka that the one who meets with death there will go straight to heaven. I suggest that the fight should be there."

Yudhisthira agreed to it willingly. And they walked towards Samantapanchaka. Duryodhana was looking very happy. The presence of Balarama was a great piece of good fortune for him. Krishna, Balarama and Satyaki accompanied them.

The fight was to begin. It was a glorious sight. They were cousins and both were the pupils of Balarama. Each was bent on killing the other. It was a great sight, but, at the same time, sad. Of the two great heroes one had to die and the world would be poorer for it.

Duryodhana said: "You can all sit down and watch this fight. It will be interesting to watch and you may enjoy it."

The fight was on. Both were strong, but it was obvious that the day's fight on the field had taken its toll and both of them were tired and so after a while they had to rest themselves. The fight was resumed and they were so evenly matched that no one could predict the result of the fight.

Arjuna was getting worried and he asked Krishna: "What do you think of this duel?"

Krishna said: "Both are good but it seems to me Duryodhana is the better fighter as he is more agile and skilled. In a righteous fight he cannot be defeated. If Bhima should kill him he will have to swerve slightly from the path of dharma. Yuidhishthira should never have let him choose his weapon. Duryodhana is fighting for his life. His technique is wonderful. But this fight has to be brought to an end."

Bhima's eyes were on Arjuna for a moment and Arjuna struck his thigh as though in admiration. Bhima understood what he meant. Bhima had sworn that he would break the thigh of Duryodhana. While the fight was going on, Bhima hit his opponent on his chest with his Gada. Duryodhana avoided the Gada by jumping up into the air. This was repeated twice or three times and then when Duryodhana leapt into the air again, Bhima hit him in his thighs.

Duryodhana had been hit by unfair means. Hitting the

thigh is against all codes of fighting. The very heavens shouted in protest at this unjust fighting. The earth was quaking. Bhima stood unmoved. He had taken an oath that he would break the thighs of Duryodhana and this was the only thought which had been in his mind these thirteen years. This was his promise to Draupadi and now, fourteen years after that momentous day in the court of Duryodhana when he had taken that oath, he had fulfilled it. He was jubilant and he rushed towards Duryodhana who was lying on the ground and he placed his foot on the head of the fallen king.

Yudhishthira ran over and pulled him away from there. He said: "Bhima, do not do it. It is unchivalrous. You have kept your word and your oath is fulfilled. Do not insult the fallen foe. Your enmity is ended. He is a king. He had at his command eleven akshowhinis and he has lost everything. I will not allow this insult to him."

Yudhishthira's eyes were full of tears. He went to Duryodhana and said: "I am innocent of what happened. I am sorry to see you like this. I salute you and bid you farewell."

Balarama was extremely angry and said: "Bhima, this act of yours is shameful. You have killed Duryodhana by foul means. This is a blot upon me also because I am your guru. I can wipe it off only by killing you."

Balarama advanced towards Bhima, but Krishna rushed to him and pulled him away. He said: "My dear brother, please do not give way to this anger. Of course Bhima has killed your dear pupil by unfair means, but then you seem to have forgotten the number of instances when Duryodhana has been unjust to the Pandavas. He forgot all about dharma when he ill-treated these brothers. The Pandavas did not want this war. I went on their behalf to Hastina and pleaded with this king to give up his obstinate refusal. But it was of no avail. To remember even one incident of those days makes me furious. I can picture Draupadi being dragged to the court of this Duryodhana. I can see Dusshasana with his hateful hands grasping her hair and trying to disrobe her. That one incident is enough for me. Can any selfrespecting man countenance such a thing? Bhima could have killed him then. His thighs should have been broken then, at the very moment when he slapped them in glee. But it was Yudhishthira's love of dharma which held them back from killing all the Kauravas.

"Bhima had to keep his oath and so he broke the thighs of Duryodhana. This one act of injustice by Bhima is enough to make you so furious as to want the death of Bhima. You were ready to kill him now. Think of me and my affection for the Pandavas! For twenty years I have been watching them. I have stood apart and seen injustice after injustice heaped upon them and I have been silent because Yudhishthira would not overstep the path of dharma. Your anger is proof that you are partial and not angry because of Adharma. You could not brook this act of Bhima because your favorite pupil was involved. I do not agree with you."

Balarama's anger against Bhima was assuaged, but he was not happy. Krishna spoke again: "My dear brother, times have changed. Kali, the fourth quarter of Time, is here and to talk of justice and injustice in fighting will be futile from now on. Time has already shown its power. The ways of Fate are indeed strange. Abandon this anger and accept that Fate is the most powerful factor in man's life."

Balarama would not be convinced. He blessed Duryodhana and after taking leave of the Pandavas he left the spot and went to Dwaraka. Krishna was unconcerned with the anger of his brother, but he was glad that he had gone away from there.

Bhima was standing as one stunned. From all around him he heard nothing but the words: "Bhima killed Duryodhana in an unfair fight." The thrill of winning the fight was all gone and it was pitiable to see him.

Bhima's oath was known the world over. He had to avenge the insult to Draupadi and the thought of this fight had been in his mind for so many years. He told himself: "Everyone knows about it. I have done only what I had sworn I would do and now everyone is blaming me for it. While fighting I had forgotten this oath. It was Arjuna who reminded me. And now he is standing as though he had nothing to do with it."

Krishna felt that he had to be comforted and cheered. He knew what a storm was brewing in Bhima's mind. He was sorry for him, so he held his hand and said: "Bhima, I approve of your action and I will not let anyone say anything against you. You have had the courage to keep your oath and I am all admiration for you." Yudhisthira looked at Bhima with affection and Bhima was shedding tears.

He fell at the feet of his brother and wept like a child. He then said: "My lord, the world is yours. Our fighting is at an end. Please accept the earth and make it yours. The chapter of hatred is closed. Draupadi need not sleep on the bare earth any longer. I have kept my promise to her. All I ask for is your blessing and affection."

Yudhishthira raised him up and embraced him with affection. The atmosphere of tension which was there because of Balarama was now cleared and everyone heaved a sigh of relief. The Pandavas could see the hurt in the eyes of Bhima and they tried to make him forget the censure of Balarama.

Krishna spoke to all of them. He said: "This Duryodhana did not listen to the advice of anyone and he has earned the reward for his sins. Come, let us go from here."

Duryodhana heard him and he replied: "Krishna, listen! Listen very carefully. You are responsible for all these acts of Adharma in this war. You talk of dharma, but then you are the one who prompted the Pandavas to resort to Adharma. You are aware that we were fighting according to the rules prescribed for a just war. The Pandavas were the ones who overstepped the rules. Today's fight was also because of you and Bhima is not to blame. I was watching you and your tactics all the time. You are the one who goaded him to hit me on the thighs. Let us go back to the war. The first casualty was our grandfather and he was killed because of you. You are the one who brought Shikhandi before him, made him throw away his weapons and then asked Arjuna to kill the old man. You made Yudhishthira speak an untruth and killed Dronacharya. Karna's killing was also unfair. Way back during the Rajasuya, Jarasandha was killed by foul means and you were behind that.

"Krishna, you are the author of all these. Yours is the sin. If they had fought by fair means, the Pandavas would not have been able to win this war. I am not a sinner, but you are. You broke all the rules in the book and you are to blame for every injustice that has taken place in this war."

Krishna's face had lost its sweet smile. It was stern and his face was suffused with anger and indignation. He said: "Duryodhana, listen to me very carefully. The sin of the destruction of the Kuru House is entirely on your shoulders. Bheeshma died because of his refusal to turn away from you and your sinfulness. Acharya Drona could easily have gone away from Hastina and lived in the forest, but he chose to remain with you and he condoned your sinfulness. Karna knew well that you were in the wrong and yet he did not lead you away from Adharma. This is the reason why they are dead. All your kinsfolk died because they did not disapprove of you and your ways. And so, their death is at your door.

"This was purely a family feud and you have the audacity to blame it on me. You seem to forget that I was the one who tried to avert the war. I asked you to be reasonable. I asked you for just five villages to be given to the Pandavas, but you were adament in your refusal. Your arrogance and your avarice were unbearable. You are the one who sowed the seeds of sin. The seeds were watered by Sakuni and Dusshasana. The fruit naturally was your destruction. I am not in the least sorry for you or your death. You deserve all this unhappiness and this death. Do not demean yourself by blaming it on others and do not try to escape blame."

Duryodhana smiled scornfully at Krishna and said: "Krishna, I have studied the Vedas. I have given away fortunes as gifts. I have done several deeds which have brought me fame and good name. I have ruled this earth wisely and well. I have tasted of all the pleasures that life can offer. All through life I have been happy. My future will also be happy. I will join my dear kinsmen and my bloved Radheya in the heavens. I am impatient to see Radheya. I was fortunate while I lived and, after death, my good fortune will continue. I am leaving this arid waste of land to the Pandavas.

"Bhima placed his foot on my head. I am not sorry for that at all. In a few hours eagles and crows will land on my head and share the spoils. This is a thing to laugh at."

The heavens rained flowers on Duryodhana while he was talking. The inmates of the heavens approved of the words of the dying king and the Pandavas had to be silent.

Krishna's anger was terrible. He said: "Listen to me, all

of you. Of course the great leaders in the army of the Kauravas had to be killed by unfair means. Bheeshma was the jewel of all Kshatriyas. It was not easy for him to be killed. It was well-nigh impossible. He could summon death when he pleased and all the many astras of the Pandavas were like pieces of straw in the presence of that great warrior. It was not possible for any of them to be killed by fair means: Bheeshma, Drona, Karna or Duyodhana. Still, for the sake of the welfare of mankind, their death was essential.

"The end justifies the means. The sin which had been committed by these Kauravas when they dragged Draupadi to the court had to be punished. I had taken an oath that I would avenge the wrong done to her. Bheeshma was there when it happened. Drona was there, but they were all silent and they did not lift up a little finger to save her from the indignity.

"They were killed by unfair means: I admit it. I did engineer it. And I am entirely responsible for the sin which clings to these killings. It was for the general good, for establishing dharma on the earth. The purpose of my life has been this and I have tried to do everything that works towards that end. I destroyed evil, protected the good and oppressed, and I have established dharma again on this earth. The earth has been cleansed of sinners like these and a new life will make mother earth happy once again. But enough of this. Come, let us go from here."

Slowly they walked away from there one by one, leaving Duryodhana lying on the ground, all alone.

Anger, the Mother of Sin

The great war on the field of Kurukshetra was at an end, but Krishna had not completed the purpose of his birth. Something more was waiting to be completed before he could go back to where he came from.

The ways of dharma are indeed mysterious and it is not possible for everyone to understand its course. Krishna used unfair means to win the war, say some. But only Krishna could do it and justify his actions. What seems to be unfair to others was right as far as Krishna was concerned. The purpose of his birth was to rejuvenate dharma which was fast disappearing and towards this end he had to work in the world of men.

He had no task of his own to perform. He was above the sphere of action. And so, anything which he did was right. Care should be taken that every man does not follow these steps which Krishna took to achieve his purpose. Man will only be a sinner if he follows Krishna in these acts. Only a man who is a Brahmavit, who is above the sway of the passions of the world, can act like Krishna.

When Krishna taught the Gita to Arjuna at the beginning of the war he asked him to concentrate on Anasakti yoga: being disinterested in the fruits of one's actions. Such a man will neither kill nor will he be the cause of any killing. This is but a reiteration of the Bhagavata dharma he spoke about.

Before his death, Duryodhana heard about the killing of the sons of Draupadi. It is surprising that even then he was happy to hear the news and he was content when life left his mangled body. Hatred is such a deadly cloak that it hides dharma from man till the end.

The Kaurava family had not given up its hatred of the Pandavas. Dhritharashtra was not able to give up this hatred. It is indeed strange that even after one has been punished for his sins, he does not bid farewell to the sinfulness in his heart. On the contrary, this feeling becomes even more violent. So punishment is not enough. Only wisdom and proper thinking will cure man of sin. Dhritharashtra was devoid of the power of thinking along the right lines and all his many losses and misfortunes could not teach him a lesson.

The funeral rites for the dead were all completed and Yudhishthira entered the city of Hastina. Dhritharashtra was burning with sorrow and anger and hatred. Yudhishthira went to him and fell at his feet and asked for his blessings. For the sake of appearances the old man clasped the nephew to his bosom and spoke words of affection. After that Bhima advanced towards his uncle. Krishna pulled him back. He quickly brought from the gymasium an iron statue and placed it in front of Dhritharashtra. This was an image of Bhima which Duryodhana had fashioned out of iron and it was a daily ritual for him to practice his Gada on this image. Krishna knew that the old king hated Bhima most as he was the one who had killed all the sons of the king.

When the image was placed before him Dhritharashtra hugged it to his bosom and crushed it to powder. After that he realized that he had done something sinful and he began to wail: "In my anger I have killed Bhima."

Krishna knew that his anger had now abated and he said: "My lord, I knew the extent of your anger and so instead of Bhima I placed the iron image of Bhima for you to embrace. Please abandon the anger against these unfortunate sons of your brother and treat them kindly. They deserve your affection and you should behave like a father towards them at least from now."

Dhritharashtra was calm. He said: "I realize my wrongdoings. I want to embrace my nephews with affection." Bhima went to him and the king embraced him warmly.

Gandhari's anger would not be assuaged by the words of Krishna. She wanted to curse all the Pandavas. Vyasa knew her intentions. He went to her and said: "My dear daughter, anger is the mother of sin. Abandon this anger and calm yourself. Your sons were slaves to sin and that is why they have been killed. Remember, when Duryodhana came to you and asked you to bless him, you said: 'Victory is where dharma is.' You knew in your heart of hearts that Duryodhana was sinful and you were aware that he would lose in the end. What happened is what you anticipated. Give up this unreasonable anger because they do not deserve your curses."

Gandhari said: "Father, I am not angry with the Pandavas. They had been used ill by my son and he is to blame. I know that. I am angry with Bhima because he killed my son in an unfair fight and he drank the blood of Dusshasana, which is cruel. This is what hurts me and makes me angry."

Bhima heard this and went to her. He said: "Mother, it is true that I was not fair when I killed your son, but there was nothing else I could do. No one can defeat Duryodhana in Gadayuddha. Indra himself will have to admit defeat at the hands of your son. In the three worlds there was no one to equal Duryodhana in valor. He was invincible. Mother, he has harassed us for years on end. I had sworn that I would kill him and so I hit him on his thighs. This was a wrong thing to do. But mother, when he insulted our queen I had taken an oath that I would do this to him. I should have broken his thighs even then, but my brother stopped me."

Gandhari said: "I forgive you for this killing of my Duryodhana. Tell me, why did you drink the blood of his brother? How could you have been so cruel?" Bhima said: "Mother, I did not drink a single drop of Dusshasana's blood. I just touched my lips with his blood. Not a drop passed my lips."

Krishna was standing with an amused look on his face. Never had he heard Bhima speak so softly and so humbly to anyone before. He stood with his palms together and Gandhari said that she had forgiven him.

Yudhishthira went to her and prostrated before her. Her

anger was still there in her heart though she had been trying to compose herself. She had bound up her eyes on the day she was married to Dhritharashtra. When Yudhishthira fell at her feet and then stood before her, from under the silken scarf she could see the nails on his feet. Her angry eyes were on them and they turned black.

Arjuna did not make any attempt to go near this lady who could kill with her look. Her tapas was so great that she was capable of burning up the entire world. Finally Draupadi fell at her feet and Gandhari was full of pity for her and her anger was all washed away by her tears. This young woman had suffered so much and Gandhari clasped her to her bosom and spoke words of affection. Each was trying to comfort the other. They had both lost their sons.

Krishna came near Gandari and again all the anger in her heart came up to the surface. She said: "Krishna, all this destruction is the result of your indifference. If you had so desired, you could have managed to avert this family feud and saved all of them from death. They say you are impartial. I do not agree. Because of your indifference, I repeat, the House of the Kurus and the Pandavas had to fight and there was this universal destruction. I now curse you. Even as this great House was destroyed by this family quarrel, your clan, the great Yadava House, will also be destroyed by a quarrel within the family. They will kill each other and your family will destroy itself."

Krishna was not angry with her. He smiled at her and there was amusement in his eyes when he said: "Mother, you have actually helped me by this curse of yours. But your accusations are all wrong. Dharma was eclipsed because of some of the heroes of this land and they were destined to meet their end on the field of battle. But the strength of the House of the Vrishnis is well known. No one can destroy them. In this entire world, why, even in the three worlds, there is no one who can fight a Yadava and defeat him. Their end can come only by a family quarrel and that you have provided by your curse. You have solved for me the final problem which was worrying me: I am grateful to you.

"But mother Gandhari, it is not fair to accuse me of indifference. You knew all about my coming to the court of your lord and you added your words to mine when your son was so obdurate. Your son was soaked in sin and his death was necessary. You knew about this end which was to come. You told him that victory would be where dharma is. You told him that he was not righteous. The Pandavas are dharmatmas.

"They have won the earth and they deserve it. Your anger and your accusation that I was indifferent are wrong. I was not indifferent. I tried my best to avert this war. Your son was a slave to his arrogance and he would not turn his face away from the path of sin he had chosen. This is the sequel to that tragic play enacted by your son and his associates."

Gandhari had to be silent when she heard the words of Krishna. She knew that he was right.

But there was still something left. Krishna had not completed his task on the earth. Thirty-six years more had to be spent on the earth before he could complete his task, before he could say that he had achieved the purpose for which he had been born.

Freedom—At Last!

Thirty-six years had passed since the end of the war on the fields of Kurukshetra. The family quarrel among the Yadavas had taken place as per the curse of Gandhari and the entire Yadava clan had been destroyed. The quarrel began over a trifling argument. They were all drunk. Kritavarma and Satyaki were talking and there was some argument about the war which had occurred so long ago. The argument became a fist fight and this in turn became more serious. People were taking sides and there was a big fight in progress before anyone could interfere. The entire clan was destroyed in no time and the Yadavas, except Krishna and Balarama, were no more.

Balarama was sorely distressed at this incident. He went to the shores of the sea and, seated there, he prepared himself to abandon his body after going into a samadhi.

Krishna thought to himself: "The purpose of my life has come to an end. It is time for me to go too."

Evening was drawing near. Krishna was lost in a reverie. He knew that the time had come when he should shed this human form of his. He sat and across the screen of his mind passed the many events in his rich and varied life. One after another they came and went and he thought of them with a nostalgic smile. Gokula, his childhood, Yashoda his foster mother, and Nanda his foster father, who were lost to him; then came the series of killings he had to take up beginning with Trinavarta. Then came Agna. The incident of the Govardhana brought a smile of mischief to his lips. How angry Indra had been! Kaliya had been sent back to the ocean. His mind hovered over the thoughts of the gopis and their devotion to him. One after another they came to his mind. He looked at each moment and dropped it.

That chapter was ended and then came Mathura. He had rid the world of Kamsa and his tyranny.

Other scenes took the place of the old ones. The Pandavas were now in his mind: their pain-filled lives and his love for them. Then came the war and the annihilation of all the many lusty Kshatriyas who were drunk with power. Duryodhana's death and the curse of Gandhari. The fight among the Yadavas on the banks of Prabhasatirtha. He had to be alive until the completion of the curse of Gandhari. He had to give life to the son of Abhimanyu. Only he could save it from the fury of the Brahmastra.

A smile of infinite sweetness spread over the face of Krishna. He remembered the incident. It was not easy to give life to that child, the only reminder of that hero, Abhimanyu. But he had been able to do it. To the end the Pandavas had been guarded by him. There was nothing left for him to do now.

Ah yes, there was just one thing he had to do before going back to where he came from. It was not impossible. He had to say farewell to Arjuna.

With the same smile on his lips, Krishna touched the mind of Arjuna with his. It was quite possible to do so. Arjuna and he were so friendly, there was such closeness between them, that they could walk into each other's thoughts.

Arjuna was in Hastina. Waves from Krishna traveled towards him and Krishna entered the mind of Arjuna. They were in tune with each other like the strings of the veena.

Arjuna was reclining in his chambers. All of a sudden he thought of Krishna. Even as he thought of Krishna, he seemed to hear the voice of his friend: "Arjuna, lie down and listen to what I have to say to you. I must talk to you."

Arjuna lay down. He went into a kind of trance. Krishna had touched the mind of Arjuna with his. He said: "Arjuna, do you remember? I had once told you that we were both born in this world to fulfill a certain purpose and that we will have to leave it once the purpose is served?"

Arjuna said: "Krishna, I remember it very well. When my chariot was burnt to ashes after the war you had spoken these words."

Krishna said: "Arjuna, the purpose of my life is completed and I have to go. Every living being, a human being or even an animal, is born with a purpose and this is the rule for all. This life on earth is a wonderful journey and it is full of meaning. What we call life is never without a purpose. It is not futile. There will be some reason for every thing, every happening in one's life. Once the reason for the birth has been fulfilled, once the purpose is served, once the horizon is reached, once the aim is realized, it is inevitable that the end should come. This is the law of nature and every living being should obey this law."

Arjuna asked: "My lord, what are you telling me? I am not able to understand what you are trying to tell me."

Krishna said: "Be brave, Arjuna. Soon, very soon, you will understand. I wanted to meet you once before I leave. We have met and I have no more desires. I am happy."

An unearthly glow could be seen on the face of Krishna. Arjuna had never seen him like this. The two friends who had been inseparable had met and parted, never to meet again.

Krishna sat down under the shade of a tree. A hunter was passing by just then. From a distance he saw something yellow and he paused. It seemed to him that a deer was there. Krishna's yellow silk and the foot which rested on his thigh created the effect of a deer standing and the hunter took aim and sent an arrow towards Krishna. The arrow pierced the sole of Krishna and the poison entered his body. The pain was unbearable and he cried out in agony.

Hearing a human voice in pain the hunter rushed to the spot and realized what he had done. He had hurt Krishna and he was scared of the consequences of his unforgivable act. He fell at the feet of Krishna and wept tears of sorrow. He was very distressed, but Krishna comforted him with the words: "My friend, do not be afraid. You have done something which is only pleasing to me. My wish is fulfilled. I had to go and I was wondering how I should do it when you solved my problem for me. I am grateful to you."

The hunter could not make out what he was saying. He only knew that he had killed the greatest of men.

Krishna abandoned his human body. The purpose of his birth had been served and he went back to where he came from. Krishna's life had come to an end. A great character had walked on this earth for a while and he had left her. Krishna has gone, but he has left behind him an unforgettable memory.

Krishna left and the sea entered the city of Dwaraka. When Arjuna came to Dwaraka there was nothing for him there. When Krishna died the Pandavas found that they had nothing left for them on the earth. They left Hastina and traveled towards the north and their destination was death.

Summing Up

This journey through life is very hard. In the course of one's life several hardships, several troubles will be encountered. There will be occasions when the mind is sorely troubled by indecision: when the doubts which crowd the mind are numerous. One is at a loss to make up one's mind as to what should be done. Gitacharya himself has mentioned this. He says: "Even the wisest of the wise will be puzzled when confronted with the problem of indecision." In another context, he says, "The path of Karma is hard."

The Upanishads speak the same truth. "The wise say that this path is as difficult to follow as it is to walk on the edge of a sword." The great wise men of the past have accepted that it is not easy to live in this world and follow the right path. When scholars and saints have found it so hard, is it any wonder then that a mere mortal is unable to make his progress smoothly through this wilderness called "life"?

How then is one to set about making this journey easy? There is but one path, one guide post. One should study the lives of great men, remember them always, and try to use them as models on which to fashion one's own life. When there is a crisis in one's life the only way to face it is to think of some character in the epics of the past and consider what he would have done. The problem will be solved and a way will be seen which will lead man out of the difficulty.

The Mahabharata is a wonderful poem. It contains

many illustrations of the workings in the mind of man. From this poem we learn a great lesson: in this creation, no one is completely good, no man can be considered to be endowed with qualities all divine, and in the same manner, no man can be considered to be entirely bad, completely devoid of goodness. Man, made of mud and air and all the elements, is a storehouse of good and bad mixed in a haphazard way.

Bheeshma, for instance, was a great character. He was a noble soul who had given up all the many pleasures of the world, who had renounced his right to the throne because he wanted to make his father happy. But even he had a fault. On the day Draupadi was insulted by the Kauravas, Bheeshma had sat silent. He did not try and stop the behavior of the arrogant princes. This will be remembered as long as the name of Bheeshma is remembered. When he was young, he had brought the daughters of the king of Kasi to Hastinapura by force and that too was not quite right. He had accepted the vow of celibacy and so this capture of the maidens was considered wrong though he did it for the sake of his brother. One of the maids was refused by all the princes and the hatred of the maid who had been spurned by all these kings was the cause of his death. The maid Amba was reborn as Shikhandi.

It is not as though Bheeshma was unaware of dharma and its many subtleties. But he was forced by circumstances to be guilty of these lapses. Why? He himself said in a few of his revealing words: "Man is a slave to wealth, but wealth does not serve any man." But no one was satisfied with these words with which he tried to justify his actions.

Dronacharya was another who was familiar with the sacred lore. But he also had not been quite honest. His mind had a leaning towards the Pandavas while his body served Duryodhana.

Karna was another unfortunate child of Fate. He was a great scholar and a hero. He was brave, generous and wise. He was deeply religious and he had a great regard for Krishna. But he had to die because of his devotion to the Kaurava prince.

If one were to cast one's eye on the many great personalities in the epics, one thinks of the rishis who succumbed to the weaknesses which beset the paths of ordinary men. The great sage Vishvamitra was no exception. His power was so great that he could raise Trishanku to the heavens with the power of his tapas and he could create a new heaven for the sake of this king of the solar race. And yet, Menaka and her winsome ways were enough to tempt him and he fell a victim to her charms, losing all the tapas he had accumulated.

Durvasa was a great sage but his weakness was anger, so much so that Durvasa and anger are almost synonyms!

Parasurama was considered to be an avatara of Narayana. But he killed his mother because his father commanded him. He brought her back to life no doubt, but the fact remains: he killed his mother.

Indra, the lord of the heavens, is not exempt from the weaknesses of the flesh! The great Yudhishthira, the symbol of dharma and righteousness, was forced to speak an untruth. As for Krishna, he resorted to a thousand tricks with but one aim: the destruction of the Kauravas.

All these examples serve to show us that no one is perfect. But it is foolish to keep noticing the faults and thinking that these great men are on the same level as we ordinary mortals. Each one of them was very great, noble and exemplary. We should learn from their great qualities and as for the faults—we should ignore them.

Fortitude is a divine attribute. We call it patience. We call it forgiveness. The man who is without this in his mental makeup, the man without compassion towards others, is indifferent towards the observance of dharma. When man becomes a slave to arrogance, this quality of compassion, tolerance, forgiveness, becomes absent in him. Treating others indifferently, without considerations, is a sin.

We have seen how Krishna strayed from the right path off and on. He had to do so. WHY? His purpose was to establish Dharma: to lessen the sufferings of the meek, to punish and, if need be, to kill the wicked. He did all this for the good of the world.

It should be remembered, and remembered carefully, that Krishna did it all without being involved in it. The path he had chosen to follow was a hard path and he could walk on this hard path, the one compared to the edge of a sword, because he was not involved in it. This is the lesson we should learn from a study of the great men of old.

By a deep study of the characters in the Mahabharata, and that of Krishna in particular, by a constant remembering of these men and their doings, by trying to emulate them, man can find it easy to walk in the path of dharma. The hardest path will be made easy by these men and their example.

Vyasa wished to make the people familiar with the Karma marga as it would be most beneficial to mankind. Karma should have but one end in view: the good of others. We should also engage in Karma with this end in view.

"Krishna" is another name for "Atma". We should realize this truth. The same Atman is residing in all living beings. This Atma cannot be split up into parts. It is all-pervading and it is one. We should realize that Krishna is not just the son of Devaki but the universal Atman which is in you and me and every one of us. He was there before he was born as the son of Devaki: meaning, he is the Paramatma, which is eternal.

He was there at the time of the Mahabharata, he was there before that and he is here now. He will be here in the future. He is eternal, indestrucible, immortal. He has no beginning and no end. Paramatma pervades everything.

We are all Krishnas. Our ancestors were also Krishnas. Our children and our descendants will be Krishnas as this entire universe is Krishna.

The story of his life is the story of the life of each one of us. When Malaviyaji said: "If you have to study the life of anyone, study the Bhagavata," he must have meant it in this sense. The lives of great men are in no way different from ours because the same Atman resides in all of us.

The waves of the sea are varied. Some are small and some are big. Some may be clean and others, unclean, laden with sand and flotsam. But they are all part of the same sea. Even so, one man may be good and meek, and another, harsh and cruel. But both have the same Atman in them and that Atman is Krishna.

Narasimha Mehta has said: "Different kinds of jewels may be wrought and given different names. But finally, when one considers the basic truth, they are all made of the same god." This is the lesson which should be learned from reading the stories of these men of old.

What I have set down is what I have tried to learn from a study of the great poems. I have not said anything new.

The acharyas have said: "Men of great intellect have heard these great truths and they have taught them to us." And so, what I have managed to gather during my studies of these poems, I have set down.

This Atma which is none other than Krishna is everywhere. It pervades everything. It has neither a beginning nor an end. It is ever young as it is eternal and it has no death because it has no birth. It is unaffected by Time or Space.

And so, I repeat, the story of great men is the story of the universe itself. Let us realize this truth. Let us salute that Krishna who is Paramatra, who pervades this entire universe, who resides in you and me and everyone.

KRISHNAM VANDE JAGADGURUM